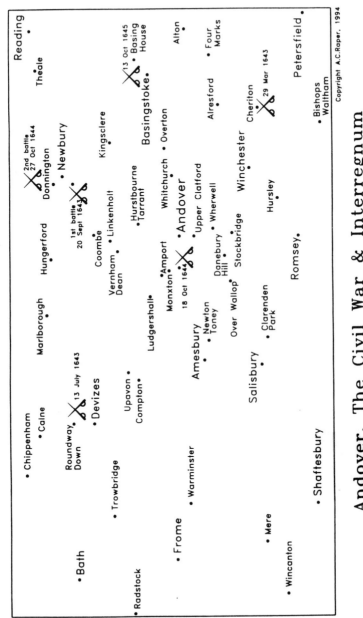

Andover, The Civil War & Interregnum

ANDOVER
The Civil War and Interregnum

by

Anthony C. Raper

Andover History and Archaeology Society
1994

First published in 1978 by Andover Local Archives Committee

Second Edition published by Andover History and Archaeology Society, 1994

© Copyright Anthony C. Raper, 1994

CONTENTS

ILLUSTRATIONS

The portraits of Charles I and Oliver Cromwell are reproduced by courtesy of the National Portrait Gallery, London. The other four portraits have been taken from the 1904 edition of Rev. G. N. Godwin, *The Civil War in Hampshire*.

PREFACE

This is the second edition of my work on the history of the English Civil War or 'Great Rebellion' and how it affected the Andover district. I am grateful for the opportunity to update and in some circumstances correct errors which found their way into the original edition. This year, 1994, is the 350th anniversary since the 'Battle of Andover', and this publication is the Andover History & Archaeology Society's contribution to mark the event.

Wherever possible I have tried to bring in a brief mention of the national events which would have affected the area and followed on with the way in which changes were brought about by those events. To fill in the missing gaps which undoubtedly happen, as Andover was not always in the thick of the fighting, I would recommend also reading a general book of the period, a number of which are listed in the bibliography.

My thanks go to George Brickell and Martin Loveridge, both now sadly departed, and to other past members of the Andover Local Archives Committee, including Bert Earney and Derek Tempero. Thanks also to the staff of the Andover Public Library and to the staff of Hampshire County Record Office. In addition my thanks to all those who contributed information since the last issue.

The words of the military historian and founder of 'The Sealed Knot' re-enactment society, Brigadier Peter Young, say everything that needs to be said:
'The English Civil War was perhaps the most important single cataclysm in our history and it behoves us to study the period from every angle.'

A.C.R.

1. THE CAUSES OF THE CIVIL WAR

Charles I was known to be an extravagant spender, constantly finding difficulties in obtaining resources to pay for his armies sent to fight the Spaniards and French in 1627 and 1628, and later the forces he led against the Scots in 1639 and 1640. In order to pay for these wars he was driven to raise money by every conceivable means at his disposal. The King demanded large sums from the House of Commons, failing to specify what he intended it for and assuming he would get what he thought was necessary, since Parliament urged that war with Spain should be undertaken.

On condition that the King did not collect 'tonnage and poundage' for more than a year, the Commons allocated him £14,000 in subsidies (Tonnage and poundage was a duty levied on imports and exports). Charles' request for funds was limited, as members haunted by the bogey of Popery wanted several specific grievances to be put to rights. Leaders in the House were convinced that favouritism was being shown by the Court to Roman Catholics. This was brought to a head when the King married a young Roman Catholic French princess, Henrietta Maria. In 1626, the King in a rage dissolved Parliament without actually obtaining what he needed from it.

His second Parliament sat in 1626 and condemned the failure of an ambitious attack on Spain organised by the Duke of Buckingham the previous year. An attempt was made to impeach him on a charge of breaching 'the fundamental laws of England', but the King answered back and arrested a critic, Sir John Elliot, and once again he dissolved Parliament. In a speech to both Houses, he gave a reminder that it was his right to call parliaments, but he would not do so if they continued to behave as they were.

Forced loans were imposed on landowners and troops were billeted on civilians because of Charles' inability to procure a grant of money. In 1627, five knights were arrested and imprisoned due to their refusal to pay the enforced loan, with the King refusing to show any cause for his actions. His resources were low, especially with two wars raging, and the unsuccessful attempt to occupy the island of La Rochelle.

By March 1628, the King, in order to obtain a money vote, called a third parliament, but once again the House of Commons refused the advancement of a grant, until its grievances were satisfied. A 'Petition of Right' embodying these grievances was drawn up and met with the approval of both the Lords and the Commons, and the King unwillingly accepted it. The Commons, not satisfied with this, went further and again tried to impeach Buckingham and also put forward a motion to make illegal the collection of 'tonnage and poundage'. This was almost the last straw for Charles; he suspended Parliament, after reminding it that he owed no account of his actions except to God.

When Parliament met again the mood had not changed, but it was now obvious that it was the King's actions that were the subject of criticism, not those of his Ministers. During the recess, Buckingham had been assassinated by a fanatic, and the demonstrations at his funeral showed the depth of feeling at the time. The criticisms Parliament made were twofold: the first relating to the illegal taxation and the second to religious policies.

Charles in spite of protests from the House of Commons defiantly appointed Arminians (who favoured the doctrine of free will above that of predestination) to bishoprics, chaplaincies and livings in his gift. Three proposals were put before the House by Sir John Elliot and were all unanimously passed after the Speaker of the House of Commons, who tried to adjourn the meeting on the King's orders, was held down in the chair. The proposals stated that anyone who introduced religious innovations and levied 'tonnage and poundage' was a 'betrayer of the liberties of England'. After this the House of Commons broke up; another one was not to meet for eleven years.

Sir John Elliot and eight other Members were summoned to appear before the Privy Council, and were later arrested for conspiring sedition. All but three were eventually released after throwing themselves on the King's mercy, but Elliot and the other two were found guilty and could be kept in prison at the monarch's pleasure. In 1632 Elliot died in the Tower of London, his harsh treatment being a sore point among the former Parliamentarians.

Peace was concluded with France and Spain, which helped reduce expenses, and an increase in his revenues encouraged Charles to govern without a parliament. An old Elizabethan tax known as 'ship money' was re-introduced, and was at first levied only on the coastal counties to pay towards the cost of a royal navy. Later in an effort to bring in more revenue, the tax was amended to include all the English counties. Public feeling was high against the levying of such a tax upon all English counties during an era of peace, and

King Charles I
by Daniel Mytens, 1631
(by courtesy of the National Portrait Gallery, London)

in 1637 John Hampden, a wealthy Buckinghamshire squire, brought a test case over the legality of 'ship money'. The verdict was for the legality of the tax, but by the narrowest possible margin.

Feelings were again aroused when Charles introduced a slightly modified version of the English Prayer Book to the Scottish Kirk. This sparked off a national resistance movement, resulting in riots in Scotland and causing Charles to try to enforce his will on his Scottish subjects by war.

Parliament was recalled on the 13th April 1640 and was asked for funds and the legalisation of 'tonnage and poundage', in order that the King might win a victory over the Scots. In a desperate effort to obtain the needed funds he offered to abandon 'ship money', but his efforts were in vain, for once again his complete offer was refused. Yet again the King dissolved the parliament, with this sitting going down in history as the 'Short Parliament'.

Charles continued his war against the Scots, without parliamentary aid, but when the Earl of Stafford's army was defeated he was obliged to accept the treaty of Ripon (21 Oct. 1640). Once again the King recalled Parliament, insisting the Scots were rebels and that funds must be provided to 'get rid of the Scots'. The Lord Keeper in his opening speech put the blame for the Scottish war fairly and squarely on the King's shoulders. Strafford was impeached at the earliest opportunity, along with Archbishop Laud, Charles' chief adviser. Strafford was executed in May 1641, after the Bill of Impeachment had been dropped and a trial under an Act of Attainder had been substituted, asserting he had severed the ancient harmony between the King and Parliament. During the readings of the Act, armed mobs gathered outside Whitehall Palace threatening the Queen, and also lined the approaches to Westminster Hall. These intimidated the King into signing Strafford's death warrant, after both Houses had unanimously passed the Act.

This undoubtedly was to lead directly to the civil war. During the first few months of 1641 a number of Bills had been passed reducing the royal prerogatives, declaring 'ship money' illegal, allowing Parliament to continue and ensuring it would not be dissolved without its own consent, and also voting money for the Scottish army. A settlement had been reached in Scotland with the Covenanters, and the Commons sent a number of Commissioners with Charles to spy on his movements. A committee was formed, so that during Parliament's recess they could keep in touch with the

Commissioners sent to Scotland, and also arrange for the demobilisation of the King's army.

Within a fortnight of the next sitting of Parliament, news reached them of a rebellion in Ireland, and John Pym and others led a group in the House of Commons which refused to consider trusting a royal nominee with the charge of an army to reconquer Ireland. This gave rise to the question of who held the ultimate power in the State. By now parties had been formed and a document outlining grievances against royal policy was passed by only eleven votes.

Charles replied by bringing an armed body of men to the House of Commons to arrest Pym and other leaders of the group, but they had been tipped off and their friends had hidden them in the City. News reached Pym that support for his cause was coming from all over the country. The King realising he had been beaten, moved from London to Hampton Court, never to return until his trial in 1649.

Civil war was now inevitable and realising this Charles ordered the Earl of Newcastle to assume the governorship of Hull, and made an attempt to control Portsmouth and the Tower of London. The Queen left England in order to obtain money for arms, with Pym making an unsuccessful attempt to stop her. In August of 1642 the King raised his standard at Nottingham and the English Civil War had begun.

"The dissolution of this government caused the war, not the war the dissolution of this government."
JAMES HARRINGTON, Oceana (1656).

2 . NATIONAL EVENTS AFFECT ANDOVER

The Search for a New England

Politics, religion and a general dissatisfaction with the state of England were causing more of the non-conformists to look for an outlet. America, in the shape of the New England states, appeared to them the most likely prospect. In their eyes, a large virtually unexplored land seemed the ideal place to practise their own beliefs, away from the 'hard line' attitude of the King. There was discontentment with the King's views on religion and of "Doctor Laud's flat Popery". The opinion of the period was that the New England states were populated by a Puritan exodus during the time of Archbishop Laud's supremacy, and were thought of by London circles as somewhat independent in spirit and not reckoned as profitable settlements. However, nearly 80,000 men women and children left for New England between 1620 and 1642.

In 1638 Peter Noyes, a senior churchwarden of Weyhill Church and also a puritan, led a party from the Andover area to Waterdown, Massachusetts in the ship 'Confidence', sailing from Southampton. He returned in early 1639 and gathered together eleven other inhabitants of Weyhill, paying a total of £76. 8s. 0d on the 12th April 1639 for the passage of himself and these people to New England. Peter Noyes later went on to found Sudbury, also in Massachusetts.

Undoubtedly others from Andover, Hants. left for the New England states and perhaps founded the many other 'Andovers' scattered over these states.

The Controversial 'Ship Money'

Ship money, a tax levied at first on the seaports, was introduced but as more revenue was required it was amended to include the coastal counties. In 1635 the tax was extended from the coastal areas to all the counties of England; there were loud protests over the whole kingdom about a tax which did not have the backing of Parliament. Responsibility for the collection of ship money was given to the sheriff of the county who in turn relied on Justices of the Peace to collect it locally.

In Hampshire the sheriff reported difficulties in collecting the taxes that were almost impossible to overcome. The Hampshire towns were assessed as follows:- Southampton £195; Winchester £190; Portsmouth £60; Basingstoke £60; Romsey £30; and Andover £50. There are frequent entries in the Andover town accounts of payments for ship money, e.g. "pd. 10sh. for 3 months tax for ye shipping money."

In May 1641, Parliament declared ship money to be illegal together with other non-Parliamentary taxes. The following January 2000 mariners from the royal navy, whom the taxes were supposed to benefit, marched into London to offer their services to Parliament.

Land and Property Tax

In order to pay for the civil war, Parliament imposed new taxes. One in particular was the 'assessment and excise tax', levied on the 'true yearly value of rent, annuities and offices', and modelled on ship money. Previously the taxes had fallen heavily on merchants and the smaller man of property. Now the tables were turning and it was the landed classes who bore the brunt of this tax. It can be said, however, that this tax was not all one-sided because the poor had to pay duties on most articles of public consumption, e.g. beer, meat, salt, soap, paper. After the Restoration it was confined to beer and spirits, cider, tea, coffee and chocolate, being luxury items. (The assessment and excise tax was to become a breakthrough in finances and it continued in use, if only in part, until the eighteenth century.)

William Blake, an Andover linen draper, was one unfortunate soul with whom the tax caught up. In 1648 he was ordered to pay a fine or composition of two years income '....... the value of the site to be reckoned as it stood before the civil war broke out' under the Land Assessment Act.

(Another linen draper member of the Blake family, Richard, is recorded as being a King's Waiter at Customs House and was forced to leave the service during 1644 owing to ill health and inability to execute his duties. Blake's position was given to another ageing merchant, Edward Roy, who had been recommended to the position by members of the House of Commons.)

Andover's Vicar Ejected

In September 1641, the House of Commons passed a Bill stating that 'it shall be lawful for the parishioners of any parish ..... to set up a lecture, and to maintain an orthodox minister at their own charge to preach every Lord's Day where there is no preaching, and to preach one day in every week where there is no weekly lecture.' Where parishes did not take advantage of this order the House of Commons stepped in to insist that ministers allow the lecturers the free use of their pulpits. The law was passed mainly to silence the Laudian ministers, and also to take away congregations from the disenfranchised, so-called 'mechanick preachers'.

Charles I in a speech, declared the lecturers to be 'Furious promoters of the most dangerous innovations' and accused them of using their prayers and sermons to incite and continue the resistance to him and his policies. This was to prove true for it was not unknown for the lecturers to act as recruiting officers and propagandists. Following the advances of Parliament's armies, those ministers with royalist political attitudes were ejected from office. Those ejected were allowed a small proportion of the parochial revenue, an amount for which their successors had to account.

An event that has not gone unnoticed in Andover's history is the ejection at this time of the Revd. Robert Clark, vicar of Andover. First reports of his 'infamous' exploits are encountered in the House of Commons Journal for the year 1642.

> "August 12, 1642. Whereas information was this day given to the House that Mr. Clarke, vicar of Andover doth obstinately refuse to obey the order of this House in admitting Mr. Symonds to preach there as Lecturer, and gives out that he, his wife and children will all be put to death before they condescend to the said order."

The Revd. Robert Clark was cited for contempt of Parliament and summoned to appear again on August 24, when witnesses were called and testified that he had given a command to lock the church doors. The vicar was alleged to have said 'Rather than Mr Symonds should preach there by order of Parliament he would lose his life, and his wife and children should die in prison; that the church was as much his own as his own house, and that he would hold his right, let the Parliament do what they would.' The witnesses' information was firmly denied, and the Revd. Clark was asked to withdraw. When he was recalled, the Speaker of the House informed the vicar that they were not satisfied with his answer, and that the statements made by the witnesses had been proved. He was then committed to the King's Bench, during the pleasure of the House, and the Lecturer, Mr Symonds, was allowed to take his position at Andover.

"Thursday, September 1, 1642, ordered that Mr. Robert Clark, upon his humble petition, expressing his sorrow that he had offended the House, be forthwith discharged from any further imprisonment."

The poor vicar suffered much humiliation by harassment and his house was often plundered and defaced. His books were stolen, those not taken were 'torn to pieces'. In defiance of the order to stop preaching, Clark was later forced to escape through a hole in the gable end of his house, lowering himself by a rope into the adjoining building. One account claims that Clark saved the Jacobean Communion ware, still in the possession of the church, by secreting it during one of the raids. On one occasion he was assaulted in the church and ran home, narrowly escaping a rain of musket shot the local soldiery fired at him.

A story which must have some basis in truth tells of how the Rev. Clarke was being chased by local soldiers under the command of a weaver of the town named Lewis and disappeared into the house of a friend. Lewis banged on the door demanding to be let in, and was horrified to be confronted by the lady to whom he had been apprenticed only a few years before. This lady had obviously had cause in the past to chastise him and no doubt put him firmly in his place on this occasion also. Lewis left the scene threatening the vicar's life and set a guard outside the house. Luck was on Clark's side for none of the guard knew him and he escaped with the help of a friend who dressed the vicar up as a mason, complete with coat, trowel and a two foot rule. His friends followed and helped him to make his escape. He was chased again whilst on his journey and forced to jump a ditch, landing badly and breaking his thigh, but he still made good his escape.

Official records of the sufferings of the Revd. Robert Clarke are scant, but a quotation from the Walker MSS kept at the Bodleian Library, Oxford states:-
"He was forced to change his place of abode four and twenty times, was imprisoned twelve times, and eleven times plundered, so that he was a sufferer

equal with his brethren, being always threadbare, and often barefoot, and must with his family have perished for want, had not the charitable interposed with their benefactions".[1]

During the period when Andover was without a permanent minister, the Parliamentary Committee put the management of church services in the hands of a blacksmith named Leggat, a brazier and a butcher, and a lock was put on the door of the pulpit to keep out 'undesirable preachers'.

The people of Andover protested and in 1649 asked the Corporation to provide a competent minister, and a letter was sent to Winchester College, patron of the church, requesting one:-

"To the Worshipfull ye Warden, Schollars and Clearks of St. Marie's Colledge neare Winton ;

The humble certificate and desires of the bayliffe, masters, burgesses and inhabitants of the Toune and Burrough of Andever;

Sheweth That ye Parsonage of Andever and Foscott is appropriate to ye Colledge and yt ye yearly value thereof is accounted at above a 1000 marks p. ann. and that the Vicaridge is now in Sequestration from Robert Clarke for his delinquency, and not sufficiently endowed for competent maintenance of an able minister, being not worth £40 p. ann.

That there is requisite an assistant for the vicar, there being 3000 souls in the said Toune and Burrough and yt a great thoroughfare for ye Westerne parts.

That the Inhabitants of the said Toune have been miserably plundered, and by losses of their Goods and Trades are much diminished.

That the Honble. Committee of Parliament for plundered ministers have ordered 50£ p. ann. for augmentacon out of the impropriate parsonage.

That the cure of Andever is totally neglected and unsupplied.

Their humble request is, that ye said Order of Committee for Parliament for plundered ministers bee redily conformed unto by yo'r Worships and yo'r Tenants: and that ye sd. Cure of Andever bee comfortably supplied with maintenance & able, godly, painful and orthodoxe ministers that Profaneness and Atheisme encrease not or so many soules under yo'r worthy charge perish not for want of being duly fedd with wholesome spiritual food."[2]

The College granted the town a minister, and a Mr Millet, then a curate of Aldbourne, Wiltshire was duly installed in Andover. A number of entries in the church registers show he was an active clergyman during the Commonwealth period. In keeping with the general trend, the minister was kept poor, and the account books show 'nine pence for mending Mr. Millet's coat.'

On hearing of the restoration of the monarchy in 1660, the Revd. Robert Clark, exiled at Northleach in Gloucestershire where he was appointed vicar, decided to return to Andover. He travelled down on Saturday, incognito, and spent the night at the house of a friend. On the Sunday morning he went into the church whilst there was a full congregation and ousted the minister, Mr. Millet, telling him 'Sir, the King has come to his own and will reign alone, and I am come to my own and will officiate without an Assistant.' The 'usurper' then continued the service giving a sermon on the 'Forgiving of Injuries' to the satisfaction of the congregation. However he could not get possession without a formal law suit in which he had to prove his induction. After just one more year in the living he resigned leaving it to Mr. Moreton, his son-in law. He died less than two years later of the gout.

False Prophet

In 1649 one William Franklin, a native of Overton but apprenticed and settled in London, somehow entangled himself in all the religious fervour associated with those troubled times, and pronounced himself to be the Messiah on his arrival at the Star Inn (now The White Hart Hotel). His travelling companion, and the person with whom he had lodged in London, was Mary Gadby and she had been honoured with the title of 'the Spouse of Christ', the 'Lamb's wife'. Other locals became involved and Goody Waterman of Clanville was proclaimed to be the 'King's daughter, all glorious within', with John Noyes of Nutbane as John the Baptist, whose duty it was to announce the coming of the false prophet into the world. Edward Spradbury of Andover was the 'reconciling angel' and Henry Dixon was the 'destroying angel'.

Somehow Franklin had conceived the idea that he had been called 'to go into the hill country, to the land of Ham' to the Star of Andover, and there to promote his wild notions. The authorities acted swiftly and arrested Franklin and his brethren. They were tried at the Winchester Spring Sessions of 1650.

William Franklin received a long period of imprisonment, Mary Gadby was flogged and others bound over to be of good behaviour. Mary Gadby assured the court that "..she companied not with him in an uncivil way, but as a fellow-feeler of her misery; at which the whole court laughed exceedingly ... A fellow feeler indeed". Franklin, a rope-maker by profession, tamely abandoned his claim to be Christ upon his arrest.[3]

Franklin was not alone in his ravings, for a certain John Robins trained himself and his followers to reconquer the Holy Land, existing only on dry bread, vegetables and water.

3 . A MATTER OF PRINCIPLES

Election of Sir William Waller

Upon the resumption of Parliament in April 1640, two M.P.'s, Sir Richard Wynn and Robert Wallop, were elected to represent Andover. This Short Parliament was soon dissolved. The King realised later in the year it was necessary to recall Parliament, when he found it impossible to obtain funds elsewhere and wanted to continue his fight with the rebel Scots. Robert Wallop was once again made M.P. for Andover, his partner this time being Sir Henry Rainsford, a man chosen for his Parliamentary leanings.

Sir Henry was not able to serve long, for in 1641 he contracted smallpox and was dead by the end of the month. An order was made to elect a replacement and Mr. Henry Vernon, a Royalist and a relation of Robert Wallop, was elected for Andover, the election being disputed by the defeated candidate Sir William Waller.

Waller then submitted a petition to Parliament claiming Vernon's seat but this was not heard until a year later. A report was made to the House on the 'State of the Election for Andover' which explained that the right of election lay with the twenty-four burgesses of the town, but only eighteen of these electors were present on the appointed day. Their votes were shared evenly between the two candidates, a casting vote being given by the Bailiff, which went to Mr. Vernon. Three other burgesses, one a declared Waller supporter, wanted to place their votes but were declared ineligible as they had not taken their oath.

It was then reported in the 'House of Commons Journal' that the House divided on party lines and decided that:-

"Mr. Vernon's Election to serve as a Burgess in this Parliament, for the Town of Andever is void. A vote was called to decide whether Sir William Waller's election be good, the voting going such:-

The House was divided.
The Yeas went forth

Sir William Waller
From an Original by Corn. Janson.

Sir Philip Stapilton   )
Mr. Jo. Moore   )   Tellers for the Yea - 107

Mr. Kirton   )
Sir Edward Alford   )   Tellers for the Noe - 102

Resolved upon the Question, That Election of Sir Wm. Waller, for a Burgess of the Town of Andevor, is a good Election: And that the Bailiff of the said Town do, at the Bar, amend the Return."

The Tellers for the Yeas represented the parliamentarians and those for the Noes the royalists. The Bailiff of Andover was then summoned to appear before the House in order that the records could be amended in favour of Waller, which he did on the 12 May 1642. Waller then took his seat, together with his other duties in the Parliamentary Army.

Sequestration of Arms

Shortly before the outbreak of the civil war the Commons made an order calling upon the Hampshire gentry to sequester any arms, etc. from those preparing to make war against the Parliament. The document is interesting for the number of Andover names it contained:

[Journals of the House of Commons, 22 July 1642]

"Whereas Informations hath been given to the Parliament that divers ill-affected Persons to the true Protestant Religion and the Peace of the Kingdom have endeavoured to prepare Horses, and Store of Arms, Ammunition, and Money with divers other Provisions, in some Parts of this Kingdom, for the assisting and encouragement of those that intend War against the Parliament: And whereas it is probable that the said Horses, Arms, or Ammunition may be brought through some part of the County of Southampton or provided there: For prevention whereof the Lords and Commons in this present Parliament assembled, do hereby require the High Sheriff of the County of Southampton and all Justices of the Peace, Mayors, Constables, and all other his Majesty's Officers, within the said

23

county to be aiding and assisting in the execution of this order; and do hereby authorize the Deputy Lieutenants of the said county, or one of them, Sir Henry Wallop, Knight, Sir John Compton, Knight, Richard Gifford, Esquire, Thomas Clark, Esquire, Thomas Chandler, Esquire, Edward Goddard (junior), Esquire, Francis St. Barbe, Esquire, Wm. Collins, Esquire, James Nutt, Esquire, Thomas Cresswell, of Heckfield, Esquire, Wm. Pawlett, Esquire, John Miller, Esquire, Wm. Bold, Esquire, John Pitman, Esquire, William Carrick, Esquire, William Withers, Esquire, John St. Barbe, Esquire, Richard Love, of Basing, Esquire, Henry Kelsey, Esquire, Thomas Hambergh, Esquire, Arthur Bromfield, Esquire, Thomas Betsworth, Esquire, John King, Esquire, Robert Knapton, Esquire, Francis Palmes, Gentleman, George Wither, of Hale, Gentleman, George Baynard, Mayor of Basingstoke and the rest of the burgesses there, Robert Harwood, Esquire, Richard Ashley, Gentleman, George Verner, of Quarley, Esquire, Wm. Blake, of Andover, Gentleman, Wm. Jervis, of Andover, Gentleman, Wm. Cooper, of Andover, Gentleman, or any of them, to make stay of all Horses, Arms, Ammunition, Money and other Provisions whatsoever, which they, or any of them, shall suspect to be preparing or carrying for the Making of War against the Parliament as aforesaid. And whereas in the Store House at the City of Winton, in the said County, there are Six Field Pieces, with double Carriages, Nine Sows of Lead, Five dry Vats of Match, with spoons, ladles and brushes, and iron bullets for the Pieces; which said Pieces and Ammunition aforesaid are belonging to the said County of Southampton. And whereas it is not convenient for the use and service of the said County that those Pieces and Ammunition aforesaid should remain and continue in the said Store House: It is therefore ordered by the said Lords and Commons, that the said Pieces and Ammunition shall be carried and conveyed into some more convenient place in the said County, as the Deputy Lieutenants, or any two or more or them shall nominate or appoint."

Ordered to Assist the High Sheriff

Another instance showing how the tensions were building up prior to the outbreak of civil war occurred on 29 April 1642, when the House of Commons considered a petition by the High Sheriff of the County of Southampton. This concerned 'obstructions and great affronts' he met with in the execution of some Orders of both Houses, relating to threatening behaviour by the Mayor of Portsmouth, and against 'some of Andevor that refused to give him assistance in conducting some rebels from the west to this town (London).'

The Sheriff was ordered to pick out 'some of the most active persons of Andevor that refused to give you assistance' which he did. At the next sitting it was ordered that 'Joseph Hincksman and William Blake of Andevor be forthwith summoned to attend this House for refusing to be assistant to the Sheriff of Southampton in the execution of an Order of Both Houses for conducting of some rebels from the west to London.'

It appears that the Sheriff, Mr. Burton, declared for Parliament well before the civil war, as the last account has shown. Again on August 11th 1642 the Sheriff endeavoured to raise the county militia for Parliament, but he was attacked by between sixty and seventy Cavaliers and about 100 persons who disliked his proceedings. The fight took place about a mile out of Southampton at Hounsdown. It may have only lasted an hour, but fifteen of the Royalists were killed or mortally wounded, the Sheriff's side losing five killed but no wounded.

Many of the locals came to assist the Sheriff, some well-armed, and at length many of the Cavaliers were captured and placed in safe keeping. The Sheriff was later thanked by Parliament for his 'good service and ready affections to the House' and ordered with his regiment to be assistant to Lord Gorges in the defence of Hurst Castle for the Parliament.

4. CIVIL WAR COMES TO TOWN

Chased Through Town

By December 1642 the Royalists began to set in for the winter at Oxford and the outlying towns and villages, content enough to play havoc with the trade routes in and out of London. In the small hours of Monday, December 5th a party of Cavaliers attacked Marlborough, taking the town from both ends of the High Street simultaneously. The defenders fought bravely from barricades and firing from the windows, but the Royalists were too strong for them. Barns, stables and store-houses were plundered; bales of cloth were taken away for the King's Army and about £200 worth of cheese. The prisoners taken were all sent to Oxford.[4] Lord Grandison was now in command of the London to Bristol road and from this position was able to divert the wool and cloth from London and strangle the trade on which Parliament's supporters depended.

Morale in the capital was low, theatres were closed, traffic was strictly controlled in and out of the city, and a monthly fast day was imposed. Demands were made on the charity of Londoners to relieve the poor, assist the victims of plunder and to help wounded soldiers and their families. The last straw came when Parliament imposed a general Assessment. This sparked off four days of disturbances against both Puritan and Royalist merchants. In the end the disturbances were dispersed by the Trained Bands. In Oxford the King made a fiery speech, denouncing Parliament's newly introduced taxes and playing on the general discontent of the city's populous.

Sir William Waller, Colonels Browne, Hurrey and Middleton and other Parliamentary forces were sent to remove the Cavaliers from Marlborough. Farnham Castle was attacked and taken for Parliament as they journeyed to their target. As Waller's army neared, the Royalists withdrew; Lord Digby went to Oxford with most of the plunder and Lord Grandison towards Basing. Waller pursued Grandison, who turned away from Basing toward Winchester when he realised that he was being followed.

The chase brought the two armies by way of Newbury to Andover and on to Winchester - "a place more likely to give him a kind entertainment, being full of malignant spirits, who indeed were not a little glad at his coming, thinking themselves now secure from danger, being under the wings of a bird of their own feather" (Vicar's Chronicle). An advance guard of horse was sent advising Lord Ogle of Grandison's coming with his six regiments and that Waller was close on his heels.

Two regiments of foot were sent to meet Lord Grandison, only to find that he had engaged the enemy near Wherwell and was busy attempting to put up a brave fight. However, the Parliamentary army proved too strong for them and after half an hour the Royalists began to retreat to Winchester. Nearly all were captured, including a brigade of horse, of whom only the officers were detained; the other ranks were disarmed and sent away, to make their own way back to Oxford.

Waller wrote of the event:-

"..we cut off two regiments, one of horse and another of dragooners, 600 of whom were gallant horse. We began our fight five miles wide of Winchester toward Salisbury way. Wherwell saw the beginning of this skirmish. The Parliament men took close order, and commenced a very hot engagement by a charge of cavalry. In half-an-hour the cavaliers began to retreat towards the city, in pursuit whereof we took fifty commanders besides Viscount Grandison, and killed divers, but the number we know not."[5]

A manuscript at Welbeck Abbey elucidates further:-

"Sir John Smith, who recovered the King's standard at Edgehill, Sir Richard Willis - 'men of undaunted resolution' - with eighteen more stood whilst Lord Grandison with other forces made good their retreat, and being thrice charged by entire troops, still bravely repulsed the enemy and broke them, in Winchester."[5]

Although in this instance there are two opposing reports we can be sure that the Parliamentary army won the day, taking many prisoners and arms. They resolved also to take Winchester and on 13th December Waller's army attacked the small force of Royalist cavalry in residence and occupied the city, just as fast as the Royalists had taken Marlborough.

In Safe Keeping

Andover was described on the 5th December 1642 as being in safe Royalist keeping, as were a large number of towns and villages over the west and south-west of England. Donnington Castle, near Newbury and Longford House, near Salisbury were two other garrisons making communication easy between Kent, Surrey and Sussex on one side, and on the other Abingdon, Wallingford, Oxford and the West.

Andover Searched

A report made by the Royalist, Sir William Ogle, in August 1643 stated that he found the High Sheriff of Southampton, Sir Humphrey Bennet, and some other gentlemen at Andover in danger, even though Lord Gerard was there with six score horse. Ogle was concerned and rightly so, for Colonel Norton, the Parliamentarian, was on his way with between 400 and 500 men and horses to draw on from Winchester and Southampton. The Royalists must have retired, for later we hear that Andover was searched and yielded four loads of match, two barrels of powder, and some fifteen muskets.

Later that evening Col. Norton's horse regiment mustered on the hill next to Wherwell where they refreshed themselves until 11pm and marched to Winchester at midnight.[6]

A notice in the Town Accounts book for this period records a purchase by the Corporation:-

"Payd Benia. Bradbourne for 1 st (weighte) of Gunpowder 0..3..0d"

Attack on Basing House

During the autumn of 1643 a new army was being raised to replace Waller's army after its defeat at Roundaway Down. It became the Southern Association made up of regiments from Kent, Hampshire, Sussex and Surrey, with a major general's commission for the commander. Whilst the troops were being raised and a decision was being made on who was to command the

Ralph, Lord Hopton

Association (for there was great rivalry for the position between the Earl of Essex and William Waller), Lord Crawford was in Alton keeping watch on the growing armies at Farnham. On the 26th October 1643 Parliamentary scouts reported back to Essex ".....that there are 1000 horse also quartered at Andever and Whitchurch and 7 collours of horse at Alton...."

Parliament agreed that the command of the new force should go to Waller, who had plans to take Winchester, which had once again been garrisoned by the Royalists. On November 3rd the Parliamentary army, now about 8000 strong, marched from Farnham towards Alton, halting at Bentley Green for an hour before continuing onward. They quartered that night at the villages of East and West Worldham, two miles from Alton. In the morning they mustered on the Winchester road at Four Marks Hill, but bad weather forced them back to their quarters. Despite the weather Waller had sent a party of horse towards Andover to keep in check Lord Crawford who was advancing from Salisbury, having previously abandoned Alton on hearing of Waller's advance. Lord Hopton too fell back to Andover from Winchester as he had not the men to deal with such a force.

On Sunday, 5th November, Waller's army mustered and continued its march towards Winchester. By late afternoon the parliamentary army halted in Alresford, about seven miles from the city, where news was received that a strong army had moved south to take them from behind. Waller, probably fearing a repetition of the defeat he had sustained earlier in the year at Roundaway Down, altered his plan and immediately ordered a march on Basing House. That night the troops quartered in the village of Chilton Candover, between Alresford and Basingstoke.

A Royalist account of Hopton's forces arriving in Andover at this time reads:-

"...But the foot which he expected, saving about 300 of his own regiment, which he brought out of Bristol, utterly fayle, which cast him into very great difficulty. But he resolved to march with what he had to Andover, where Colonel Gerard with his brigade was then quartered. Depending upon his intelligence for the state of the enemy in that country, he came as he had designed, into Andover three or four hours within the night, and there kept his men in guard (sic), till he had consulted with Lord Gerrard, who came immediately to join him at his lodging, and the Earle of Craforde with him. The Lord

Gerrard presently assured him that Sir William was that night come into Alsford (six little miles from Winchester) with a formidable army, reputed to be about 5000 foot, and between 2000 and 3000 horse, and a good Trayne of Artillery, and that he resolved to advance to Winchester the next day."[7]

The Parliamentary army marched to Basing on November 6th, where Waller received fresh information telling him that danger no longer threatened. At daybreak on the 7th the attack on Basing House began, but the garrison fought back bravely, their only gun "..slew a large number of the enemy". The Cavaliers then 'fired' all the houses which could provide cover for the assailants. Fighting continued for three days until Waller withdrew his men to Basingstoke on the 10th to plan another attack. The attack never came however, for on the 11th he received news of a large concentration of Royalist forces at Winchester under Lord Hopton. There were three alternatives open to Waller: firstly to meet the enemy and fight, secondly to march to Winchester and attempt to take the city, and lastly to retire to Farnham and await further supplies. At an officers' meeting the first proposition was carried, but the officers returning to their regiments were faced with a mutiny so Waller decided to retire to Farnham.

Late in November Lord Hopton decided to consolidate his forces and withdrew his outposts from Odiham, Basingstoke and Long Sutton. At the same time he posted Lord Crawford and Col. John Bolle's regiment at Alton, and quartered most of his foot at Winchester, Andover, Petersfield and the surrounding villages - he considered Basing House was 'well able to take care of itself'. It was at this time that Hopton "summoned all Hampshire men, between the ages of sixteen and sixty to appear in arms for the King at Winchester."

Fortified Post at Weyhill

Lord Hopton, the Field-Marshal of His Majesty's Western Forces, was reported on 17th January 1644 to be planning to place guns and a fixed camp in a commanding position upon 'Warhill' or Weyhill. Three such posts were to be established enabling ease of communication with the King at Oxford, who at this time was intending to open his parliament there. The first of these fortified posts was to be at Winchester, with another at Weyhill and a third at

Reading, a distance of some fifteen to twenty miles from each other. Operations were greatly impeded by hard frosts and heavy falls of snow, forcing Hopton's forces to stay in Winchester bickering with the cavalry of Prince Rupert over food and supplies.

No record exists as to the gunpost ever being erected, but whether it was or not, the King pressed ahead with his parliament and opened it on January 22nd at Christ Church Hall in Oxford.

Stragglers Taken (13 March 1644)

William Balfour, Major-General of Horse under Sir William Waller, whilst marching from Reading to Devizes, took a few straggling Cavalier horsemen who were billeted in Andover. From here Balfour marched on to Newbury, which had at that time a garrison of 5000 horse and foot.

It may only have been coincidence, but the same day a Royalist attack was made on Romsey, which had but a month earlier been in Parliament's hands. About 80 officers and foot soldiers were taken prisoner and moved to Winchester for safe keeping. They were not kept prisoner for long, however, as Parliament occupied the city after the Cheriton battle. It could be that the Romsey attackers were the force Balfour had missed as he fell on Andover.

5.   THE BATTLE OF ANDOVER

Preparations for Cheriton

On March 21st 1644 the Royalists were once again in Andover; this time it became the headquarters of Lord Forth's cavalry. From here he awaited reinforcements from Oxford and provisions from the Sheriff of Berkshire. The next day an order was made for a week's supply of hay, oats or peas for Lord Forth's cavalry to be sent "with all possible diligence to Andover" and "from thence Lord Hopton is to take order for carriages to bring it to his quarters." Lord Percy was ordered to send to Hopton 50 barrels of powder, 6000 weight of match, and "bullet proportionable to the powder". "Carriages are there very scarce and hard to be gotten."

Cheriton

To the Roundheads it must have seemed that things were warming up, especially when Lord Forth joined forces with Hopton and Wilmot near Alresford on March 27th. Between them they had about 5000 horse. Sir William Waller had earlier intended taking Basing House, but Sir Richard Grenville, one of his most trusted commanders deserted and rode to the King at Oxford, giving away details of Waller's plans. Forced to abandon his attempt, Waller moved his army toward the Royalists grouping at Alresford.

On the morning of Friday, 29th March the London regiments of the Parliamentary army advanced on a Royalist outpost in Cheriton Wood, but they were driven back by heavy gunfire. The Royalist cavalry seeing them retreat charged down upon them, but Sir Arthur Hazelrig came to the help of the retreating armies, engaging the Royalists and driving them back. More Royalist cavalry came to their aid and were soon involved in a desperate bloody battle, in a narrow lane where they found difficulty in manoeuvring.

Retreat from Cheriton

The battle did not go well for the Royalists. Sir Henry Bard's regiment was destroyed, and when Sir Edward Stawell was wounded and taken prisoner, his regiment turned and fled. A Royalist eye witness described the scene when Colonel John Smith charged the Parliamentary army; "..their Canon, when he come almost within pistol-shot to charge in, flies off so freely that it amazes his horses." As his horse reared and turned sideways, so a cuirassier (a heavily armoured soldier) shot him on the left side below his armour. "With this wound he falls, and with him the fortune of the day and the courage of our horse. All ran away almost except his own troop" who rescued the Colonel together with his horse and arms. The cuirassier who shot the Colonel was himself shot in the eye by one of Smith's lieutenants.

The Colonel's wound did not bother him at first and he and his men retired to Wonston, a village five miles north of Winchester, where his troops were quartered. Overnight the Colonel lost a great deal of blood and by morning he was greatly weakened, but did not wish to appear so to his troops. An eye witness, Edward Walsingham, a soldier in Smith's troop, relates the story:-

"...and so to Oxford if it were possible. He not withstanding his deadly wounds, comes downstairs on foot, and ascends the carriage. When we drew neare Andover he began to say (his senses being a little astonished) 'Good my Lord let us charge them once again and the day is ours.' As soon as we entered the towne he began to invoke the sacred name of Jesus often repeating it with a gust and sweetnesse in the divine vertue of it. Shortly after, over and against the signe of the Angel, in a mild repose he expired where it would have grieved the hardest heart to have seen him round enclosed with sundry gentlemen, condoling with teares the untimely end of so Feerelesse a Gentleman". [8]

Colonel Sir John Smith's body was later removed and given a stately funeral at Oxford on 1st April 1644.

After Cheriton

After a day's rest the Parliamentary army mustered, and that night (30th March) marched to Stockbridge. The next day, after receiving intelligence reports that about three hundred of the enemy lay at Andover, they were ordered to fall on the town. On arrival they found the enemy had already left, leaving behind only a few stragglers. Not content with only these, they followed the Royalists as far as Newbury. After a rest they marched back to

Andover arriving there on the 2nd April, and leaving again on the 4th for Stockbridge.

Whilst in Andover, Sir William Balfour was informed that Lady Hopton had reached Newbury on her way to join her husband, who was now recruiting reinforcements in the Oxford area. Sir William promptly dispatched a party of horse to Newbury and succeeded in surprising Lady Hopton, together with her escort of 200 men, two coaches and twelve coach horses. "Order was given to treat the lady with the respect due to her quality and she was quickly dismissed, and conveyed to Oxford, being permitted to take with her what plate and jewels belonged to her or her attendants, but the rest was made prize of".

The Cheriton battle did much to increase Sir William Waller's reputation which had suffered when his army was destroyed on Roundaway Down by Prince Maurice's and Lord Hopton's forces. London was therefore overjoyed at Parliament's successes in Hampshire, and it did not object quite so strongly when pressed for more money and help. Waller was back in favour again and was ordered to recruit three thousand foot and seventeen hundred horses and dragoons for his army. It was intended to attack Oxford whilst the Royalists were still in a state of confusion.

Sir William stopped over in Andover again on the 9th April 1644 on his way from Winchester to pick up supplies at Farnham.

By May plans for the Parliamentary army to attack Oxford were well under way, while the Royalists were still in a weakened state. The King mistakenly decided to make the Oxford army more 'nimble' in the field by withdrawing from Reading and Abingdon. However, this left these towns free to be occupied by enemy troops, which was soon the case. This action forced the King's cavalry out of Berkshire, leaving Oxford open to attack.

The Earl of Essex, amazed by the King's conduct, co-operated with Waller and together they planned a serious attack. Essex placed his forces east of the city whilst Waller's forces positioned themselves to the south and west, leaving the north as the only route for escape.

During one of Waller's interviews with Essex, it was decided that he should post a detachment at Andover "with a view of checking the advance of any relieving army from the west." (18 May 1644).

Attack on Basing House

Another attack was to be made on the King's loyal supporters at Basing House during June that year. For eighteen weeks the Parliamentary army under Colonel Norton attacked and repulsed attacks from the garrison. Even after a party of Cavaliers from Oxford had managed to relieve the besieged house and capture stores in the process, a further counter-attack was made. The attackers again closed tenaciously around the house but were unable to take it until Cromwell's attack on it in October 1645.

In his book *The Civil War in Hampshire* Godwin writes:-
"Colonel Norton himself was on June 15 (1644) daily expected to return to Basing, having gone with his regiment of horse a week previously to Andover, which was said to be occupied by the King's forces."

Royalist Plunder

'I had six oxen t'other day,
And them the Roundhead stole away;
A mischief be their speed.

I had six horses left me whole,
And them the Cavaliers have stole,
I think they are both agreed.'

The words of this old song illustrate the fact that both sides were as bad as each other when it came to looting and plundering.

On Sunday, 30th June 1644 Sir William Ogle, governor of Winchester Castle, hearing of a wagon train on its way to London, sent out a detachment to capture it. The force, consisting of 50 horse, 60 musketeers and 40 pikemen, marched toward Andover to intercept the convoy as it passed by the town. The cavalry entered the town, whilst the infantry halted at a distance of some three miles.

The Cavaliers took possession of sixteen waggons laden with cloth, cheese, oils etc., 60 or more oxen and 36 horses on their way from Wiltshire to London. With this plunder valued at around £10,000 and with cloth useful for trade abroad, the Cavaliers retired unmolested to Winchester.

The Battle of Andover

After the success at Oxford, Essex and Waller met to discuss the best way of completing the King's discomfiture. Waller reluctantly agreed to stay in the Midlands and follow the retreating King. The Earl of Essex, however, perhaps a little jealous of Waller's recent successes, marched westward with the aim of relieving the besieged town of Lyme and he also hoped to cut off the advance of the Queen's army at Exeter. But he had hardly set foot towards Lyme when he received letters from Waller urging him back so that together they could settle with the King in a couple of days. Essex did not return, but continued with his march leaving Waller to his own devices.

This gave the King a chance to gather fresh breath, and after gathering new recruits and provisions on his journeys, he turned as if to march on Oxford. The Cavaliers met Waller at Cropredy Bridge and after a battle Waller drew off having sustained heavy losses. The King decided to join his wife for there was very little now to stop him from doing so. This left Waller with a demoralised army whose men were deserting fast.

News came back from the West, and on 18th August 1644 the Committee of Both Kingdoms was advised that Sir Thomas Fairfax, the Lord General, was in difficulties, surrounded by four armies and in great want of provisions. It was decided that Sir William Waller should go into the West with a body of horse and dragoons.

Sir William set off on the 7th September with only 2000 foot, 800 horse and 150 dragoons, for that was all he could muster, owing to the lack of co-operation between the Southern Association and local commanders in Wiltshire

ROBERT DEVEREVX EARLE OF ESSEX HIS EXCEL
lency &c Generall of yᵉ Army

and Dorset. Even with these difficulties, Waller's army joined up with the army of Lt. General Middleton near Taunton and that of the Lord General's horse, which had broken through the Royalist cordon at Lostwithiel.

Waller and his troops remained in Wiltshire and Dorset for the next month, strengthening the south coast garrisons with his infantry. Realising that all his men would not be enough to attack the King, Waller urged the Committee to send more troops. The Earl of Manchester, often at loggerheads with Waller, was ordered to Oxford to fill the gap left by Sir William's march westward. Manchester did not seem keen to comply for on the 27th September his army still lingered in Middlesex. The Committee of Both Kingdoms feared the King would march on London and so ordered Manchester to send his cavalry ahead to join that of Essex and Waller at Shaftesbury. At the same time the rest of his foot would rendezvous with Essex's re-equipped infantry at Newbury. Manchester was slow in replying for he was still at Reading during mid-October, and it was not until the King's army was at the Hampshire border that he marched to join the army of the Earl of Essex.

Waller now received orders to fall back towards the combined armies of Essex and Manchester. After marching through Salisbury, Waller ordered his 3000 horse and 1500 dragoons to halt at Winterbourne Stoke near Amesbury; he was still there on October 15th when he heard that the King was nearing Salisbury. Sir William then fell back to Andover, still a considerable distance in advance of the combined armies.

Meanwhile in Salisbury, the King and Prince Maurice hatched a plan to attack Waller at Andover. Lord Goring urged the plan forward and the date was set at the 18th October 1644. In order to stop his plan being leaked to the enemy, the King posted guards on all the 'avenues' out of the city that night.

On the 17th October in Andover a court martial was held by Sir William Waller at a Council of War.

"Andover, 17 October, 1644.
"Whereas Major Edward Wood once Agitant Gen of the foot to Sir Willm Waller is now accused for killing one Thomas Pritchard then under the Comand of one Captaine Knapp of the Regiment of Col: Houblon. In as much as the aforesaid Thomas Pritchard is proved to have been the chiefe actor and Incourager of a dangerous Mutiny at Basingstoake, not only by resisting and affronting the sayd

39

Major at the time injoyned and sent to suppresse the sayd Mutiny, It is ordered by the joynt consent of the whole Councell of Warr, That the sayd Major Edward Wood shall stand aquitted as concerning the death of the sayd Thomas Pritchard, In that it did appeare that what the Major then did was in performance of his duty. It is ordered this day by the Councell of Warr that Andrew Fyan, for that (according to his own confess'on) hee wounded his Leift., shal be harquebuseered to death."[9]

The next morning, October 18th at seven o' clock the King's army mustered at Clarendon Park, although the foot under Prince Maurice did not arrive until eleven, delaying the march until noon that day. The King's advance guard came within four miles of Andover, probably around Amport or Monxton, before Waller had any indication of their whereabouts. Sir William's response was to muster his army, about three thousand and order them to the outskirts of Andover as if he meant to fight. But seeing the large force the King was commanding, Waller withdrew through the town, leaving behind a strong party of horse and dragoons to cover his retreat.

Seeing this, the King's vanguard charged and "..routed them with good execution, and pursued them through the town, and slew many of them in the rear, until the darkness of the night secured them and hindered the others from following farther". Fighting lasted around two hours, in which time about eighty prisoners were taken in an area of about two miles. Of the prisoners captured one was William Carr, a Colonel in Waller's Army, another was a Captain "...a Scot, that died, who a little before his death rose from under the table, saying he would not die like a dog under the table, but sat down on a chair and immediately died of his wounds".[10]

The King quartered for the night at the 'White Hart' Inn at Andover. (This was later known as the Star and Garter and now the Danebury Hotel. It was common practice for the landlord of each public house to take the name of the building with him wherever he moved and during the Civil War period the present 'White Hart' was known as the 'Star Inn'.)

The 'battle' is said to have taken place in a lane leading into Andover, in the region of the later Andover Airfield, or Red Post Bridge. About thirty of Waller's men were killed and about ten to twenty of the King's (although there is some ambiguity as regards figures between the chroniclers).

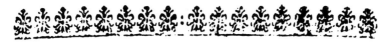

MERCVRIVS AVLICVS,

Communicating the Intelligence and affaires of the Court, to the reſt of the KINGDOME.

The 42 VVeeke, ending Octob. *19.* 1644.

His Majeſty ſtaid at *Salisbury* Tueſday night, Wedneſday, & Thurſday, and on Friday advanced towards *Andover* in *Hampſhire* where the Rebells lay, with intention to ſtoppe His Majeſties motion ; ſomewhat ſhort of *Andover* a Fore-lorne hope being ſent out, met with another of the Rebells very neare their maine body; both charged & kept their ground, till two bodies of His Majeſties Horſe came up and marched into the field, where the Rebells ſtood ; at ſight whereof the Rebells forces began to fly out at the other end of *Andover* Towne ; yet made not ſo good ſpeed, but that His Majeſties horſe overtooke them, and ſlaſhed them ſoundly, eſpecially in a Lane entring into the Towne, where that body of Rebells was routed, and very good execution done upon them, perſuing them through *Andover* a good way beyond, till the darke night ſtopt further perſuit. Which done, His Majeſty marched into *Andover* and lay there all night: This Morning He advanced towards *Whitechurch*, and ſent the Earle of *North-ampton* with his owne Bragade of horſe to viſit Maſter *John Fines* at the ſiege of *Banbury* Caſtle, where Sir *William Compton* (his Lordſhips Brother) hath ſo handſomly entertained Col. *Fines*, that upon the gallant Earles approach Mr *Fines* will follow his own Fathers example but not his inſtructions, as you ſhall heare next Weeke under his Fathers owne hand.

FINIS.

At Longleat House in Wiltshire there is a painting of the Earl of Lauderdale, a Scottish emissary on King Charles' side and later a member of the famous CABAL. Underneath the painting are the words 'John Maitland, Earl of Lauderdale wounded at 'Battle of Andover' 1644'.

On Saturday the 19th the Royalist army mustered and marched on, stopping for the night at Whitchurch, and then on to relieve the sufferers of Donnington Castle at Newbury. According to the *State Papers - Domestic*, King Charles slept the night of the 19th at the house of Mr Richard Brooke of Whitchurch.

On the 19th October the Earl of Manchester wrote from Basingstoke:

"Yesternight late I received a very hot alarm (from) Sir William Waller's quarters, that the King with all his army, was come to Andover, and that he was upon his retreat towards me, whereupon I drew out my foot and those horse that were with me in order to help Sir W.Waller who reached Basingstoke with little or no loss."[10]

Waller in his *Experiences* writes his account of the event:

It was a great mercy of God, that when the King came suddenly upon me with his whole army att Andover and I had then nothing but a mere body of horse and dragoons with me, I made a fair retreat to Basingstoke".[11]

There are several references made to the incident in the town records, especially those of burials of soldiers, generally from the inns, viz. "a stranger from ye plow" (now the Southampton Arms), "Ye Starr", etc. In addition there is a note in the Town Accounts of a gift from the Corporation of Andover to Sir William Waller during his short stay:

"1644 Payd Mr. Jarvis for a Sugar loafe given to Sir Willm Wallor 0..13s..4d"

Recently physical evidence has come to light of the 'Battle of Andover' during a metal detector survey in a field west of Monxton village. A number of cannonballs and a considerable quantity of musket balls were uncovered in addition to a stirrup and various chains.

6. ROYALISTS CAPTURED IN ANDOVER

Goring's Cavalry Quartered in the Town

The Royalist hold was still strong in the south. Newbury remained in Royalist hands despite an attack by Manchester and Essex; Prince Rupert was also able to relieve the garrison a little later. Lord Goring had his headquarters in Winchester, but some of his cavalry were quartered in Andover. From here, on 9th January 1645 Goring's cavalry made a raid on Farnham, mainly to scare and spread alarm rather than for any territorial gain, and they returned to Andover again the same day.

The attack did not hamper the progress of the Parliamentary forces, and we hear later of 1500 horse from Kent and a strong force from Reading amassing there. This force, under Waller, had intended to capture Winchester, but on the night prior to the assault a trumpeter defected and warned the garrison and the scheme had to be abandoned. On February 12th, on hearing that three regiments of Goring's horse were quartered in Andover, Waller sent a party to beat up their quarters; but once again warning had been received and the Cavaliers retreated to Newton Toney, near Amesbury.

Royalists Captured

Lord Goring was now a serious threat in the West; Weymouth was taken for the King and the fortress of Bristol too, placing Parliament in an awkward position. Taunton was now at the centre of a Royalist controlled area and so it was decided that both Sir William Waller and Oliver Cromwell should go to the relief of the Parliamentary garrison. Operations to go to their rescue were hampered; Waller awaited arms, knapsacks and stockings for his men, and a regiment mutinied at Portsmouth; seven hundred men marched back to their old quarters. Westminster ordered Cromwell to join them with a thousand pounds of pay, to try and restore order.

On the 4th March 1645, Waller and Cromwell were given instructions to march into the west with their cavalry "...all excuses set aside". Three thousand horse and dragoons of Waller's, together with Cromwell's command, rode from Owslebury to Andover on the 8th, where they surprised a small party of Cavaliers under the command of Lord Percy. Waller recorded the event in his *Recollections*:

George, Lord Goring

"When I tooke the Lord Piercy att Andover, having att that time an inconvenient distemper, I desired Collonell Cromwell to entertaine him with some civility; who did afterwards tell me, that amongst those whom he tooke with him (being about thirty), their was a youth of so faire a countenance, that he doubted of his condition; and so to confirm himself willed him to sing; which he did with such a daintiness that Cromwell scrupled not to say to Lord Piercy that being a warriour, he did wisely to be accompanied by Amazons; on which that Lord, in some confusion, did acknoledg that she was a damsel; this afterwards gave me cause for scoffe att the King's party, as they were loose and wanton, and minded their pleasure more than their Country's service, or their Maister's good."[12]

It was found that some of Waller's prisoners had been released from service to the King upon a promise to retire to France. An old pass for France was produced, which was allowed, and the prisoners were released to continue their journey. One member of the party, the Earl of Sussex (Lord Saville), defected to the Parliamentary side, who nevertheless declined to trust him. Waller's troops were described as "..a well disciplined and orderly army, that behave themselves with all civility to the people and gain much love".

On the 10th March the parliamentarians marched on to Amesbury where they quartered for the night. Scouts reported that a party of 400 Cavaliers were on the march, and they planned to stop at Devizes. Next day, the combined armies of Cromwell and Waller marched towards the town. As they neared it Cromwell took his army and fell in on the Bath side of town, whilst Waller carried on. On Wednesday, Waller drew up his forces on the town catching the Royalists off guard. They retreated toward Bath, where Cromwell's men lay in readiness - it was all the Cavaliers could do to offer a token resistance before they were taken.

Waller Resigns

By March 1645, Lord Goring had given up all hope of advancing towards London, and was forced to retreat into the West. He launched an attack on the strong Parliamentary garrison at Taunton, but his troops could make little headway. Waller's and Cromwell's troops were by now attacking various

Royalist positions throughout the west country. Waller had made repeated attacks on Royalist quarters on the Wiltshire-Somerset border, but after an attack on Goring's headquarters at Bruton news was received that a long awaited bill had been passed by the Lords which required politicians who held a military position to resign. The names of both Waller and Cromwell were on a list drawn up by Parliament, requiring them to resign their commands at Windsor on 17th April 1645.

Sir William fell back to Andover with almost all his horse and dragoons around the end of April, on his way to resign his command. Cromwell, however, was given a reprieve, as recent movements of the King at Oxford were causing Parliament some concern, and it was decided that he should take the field yet again.

Council of War

Another bill passed at the same time as the Self-Denying Ordinance was one requiring the organisation of a better army, which became known as the New Model. Sir Thomas Fairfax was chosen Commander-in-Chief, with Oliver Cromwell as his General of the Horse. The New Model's first task was to be the relief of Taunton, which was once again under siege by Lord Goring and the young Prince Charles, whom the King had made Captain-General in the West. Goring abandoned the siege before Fairfax even set out for the town, and Fairfax's orders were changed to lay siege to Oxford. Even so, Fairfax sent a reasonable force to relieve Taunton, keeping the rest to take the city of Oxford.

On the afternoon of May 4th 1645, Fairfax's army marched from Newbury and the seven infantry regiments, about 11,000 strong, quartered that night in Andover and the neighbouring villages, awaiting the cavalry. The next day a general muster was called a mile out of town on the Salisbury road, probably near Red Post Bridge. During a wait of two hours or so, a council of war condemned five men to death. Four of the condemned were authors of a mutiny in Kent, the other was a renegade or deserter. Three of the men were hanged outside Andover (a 'Gallows Field' is named on an early map of Red Rice estate, near the Red Post Bridge). The other two, a mutineer and the deserter, who was a parson's son and a native of Wallop, were executed upon a tree at Wallop, and left in the way of the army's march to act as a warning to any other would-be offender. A chronicler records that "..Both of them died as they lived, like sots."

On the following day (6th May) it was proclaimed throughout the army that it meant death for any man to plunder; nothing was to be taken without payment, as all ranks had just received four months' pay.

Cromwell's Brigade Arrives

On the 20th September of that year, Cromwell with his men was in Andover, using the town as a base from where he could attack the Royalist garrisons of Winchester and Basing. Devizes, which had been taken again for the Royalists, surrendered to him on the 22nd without loss of any man, and a number of prisoners were taken.

The commanders of the City horse and dragoons were ordered to convey provisions from Andover on the 22nd September, and then march into Sussex to quell the Clubmen. The Clubmen rose in Wiltshire, Dorset, Hampshire and Sussex and rebelled against both Roundhead and Cavalier alike, aiming to fight off soldiers who tried to take their food, money and provisions. Their ranks included yeomen and farmers and were often led by the lesser gentry (sometimes clergy), fighting with cudgel and pitchfork against the sword and musket of the soldiers.

Richard Blake

September 1645 was election time in Andover and two men were nominated for the post of Bailiff. Richard Blake was elected to the position on the 8th and was given a day to consider accepting it. The day passed without answer from Mr. Blake; several of the approved men were also missing from that council meeting as the minutes show:

"27 September 21 Charles (1645)
Whereas Mr Richard Blake standeth Baylife elected for this present year & hath had notice thereof & sufficient warning to come and take his oath for th'executinge of the office of Baylife & hath not yet done the same it is therefore ordered this daye that he shall come

in some tyme before tomorrow night & take the said Oath & the other Oathes beloninge to a baylife of this Corporacon to take the wh. if he shall not doe, he is fined one hundred pounds & adjudged & contempned to the prison there to laye and remayne untill he shall have paid the said fine & taken the oaths aforesaid. It is alsoe ordered that those of the approved men that were warned to be here this daye & have not appeared that they are fined 6s 8d p. piece."

The unwilling Blake appeared before the council the same day and was sworn in as Bailiff.

7. FIRE IN ANDOVER

Riots Around Andover

By the autumn of 1645 the end of the war was in sight, thanks mainly to the successes of the disciplined New Model Army. New units were being raised for the push into the west and to fight in Ireland. Col. Jephson, a local landowner and M.P. for Stockbridge, was given the task of raising a regiment of horse for that purpose in August. However, the men could not be shipped to Ireland straight away and they were employed in the reduction of Basing House the following month.

During November they were employed in conveying infantry to Reading, but as the weeks passed their pay fell into arrears and by December they were beginning to grow restless. Their enthusiasm to serve in Ireland evaporated and according to the testimony of William King and his wife of Upper Clatford "..they intended no such matter." The soldiers blamed the County Committee for Hampshire for not paying them, as the testimony of Mr and Mrs King continues: "..if they would meet any of the committee anywhere out of Winchester they would from them their clothes, horses and monies."

The men were true to their word for Gabriel Floyd, the servant of John Marks, collector of sequestrations for the Andover division, was seized and plundered by a troop of Jephson's horse under the command of Major Gifford, whilst on his way to meet his master at Longparish. When Marks went to investigate he was called a rogue by the Major and robbed of all his linen and money and was kept prisoner for half-an-hour despite his protests.

But according to the King family's testimony it was not only the officials who were liable to be plundered for the soldiers robbed people coming from Collingbourne Fair: "..one poor man of his horse and others of their monies." The County Committee wrote to Speaker Lenthall in Parliament, expressing their concerns and resentments, complaining of the "outrages, pressures and plunders" of the soldiery. They drew to the Speaker's attention the complicity of officers like Major Gifford and begged some relief.

Six weeks later, on 15th January 1646, the Commons gave the order to rectify the situation and made provision for £1746.15s.8d. to be supplied for "the speedy sending away" of Jephson's regiment to Ireland. At the same time, they ordered the Hampshire Committee to pay a further £504.6s.0d to the regiment, the arrears for its service against Basing House the previous autumn. Furthermore the Committee was ordered to compensate those that had suffered from the soldiers' demands for money. However, the Committee of Both Kingdoms were still urging Jephson "to expidite the shipping away of your horse into Ireland" on the 10th February.

New Model Army

Crediton was taken, Tavistock had been stormed and recruits flowed to Parliament's cause. The Royalist general, Lord Hopton, fought on despite decreasing enthusiasm and diminished supplies, but eventually found it necessary to admit defeat. On the 14th March 1646 at Exeter, Hopton signed articles of surrender, thus leaving the way open for an assault on the Royalists' chief centre of defiance, Oxford.

Plans were made, and Fairfax marched his victorious New Model Army into Andover on the 25th April 1646, on their way to attack the Royalist 'capital'. After a halt of about two days in Andover they proceeded to Newbury, from where he sent an advance party of horse to threaten the city. Charles had been having secret negotiations with the Scots and upon hearing of the enemy's advance, decided his destiny lay with the Scots; he escaped from Oxford on the 27th April in disguise, reaching the Scottish army at Newark on the 5th May. Oxford finally surrendered to Cromwell's forces on the 20th June.

Whilst the Parliamentary army rested in Andover, one soldier took his daughter to be baptised, as the parish records show:-

"Isbell daughte to James Hepperbe soldier of Sr. Tho farfax army"   25 Ap. 1646.

Fire

In 1647 a great fire broke out along the west side of the Upper High Street, making 82 families homeless. It is thought that the whole of the west side from the Guildhall up to the former 'Baldocks' (69/71 High Street) was destroyed right back to the river. Winchester College owned most of the property burnt down and granted the families who lost property a total of £5. One man, Robert Mountain, who lost property valued at £800, received the sum of £1.

The town's Charity Chamberlains also deemed it necessary to relieve the stricken.

"It. Paid the Churchwardens and Overseers decem the 10, 1647 .. .. 10 li.0.0."

The fire remained in the memory of the townsfolk for years afterwards as many entries in the town's court and accounts books show. In the 'Presentments by the Jury' in 1649, townspeople were reported for making fires in their houses without the use of a flue or chimney.

4 Oct, 1649 - "We present Richard humber, William Scullerd tenants to the Wido Douse, Peter Oldene, Wido Cooke, Wido Freake, John Myller, Jho. Thurman, Richard Pontyn, Wido Sutton of Charleton, for making a fier agaynst a wall without Chimney or Flew, which is very dangerous. James hart of Wyldeherne all thus having very dangerous flewes, also Jno, Butler - to be amended between this and Lenards tide under penalty of xxs."

In the Presentments by the Jury dated 1649 is another item:

'Item we present the want of the Toune Ladder, Crrokes and Buckets, to be considered immediately.'

Once again on the 18th January 1650 the Corporation ordered that "..none shall thatch any house or howses in or next to the high streete in Andever" under a penalty of £10, as yet another measure to guard against a recurrence of 'the great fire'.

Leather tanning was an important industry in the town and in order to safeguard the industry and the town, the Corporation in 1688 ordered the removal of the East Kilns to the river.

"Whereas by sad experience it hath been found that the East Kilnes which are erected and used by the tanners of this town are very dangerous and have been several times very likely to have set the whole Town on fire. It is therefore ordered that before the Feast of St. Michael next ensuing all the Tanners of this Town shall remove all the East Kilnes to the Water side and sufficiently tile them, there to remain to prevent future danger upon pain of 40s. not obeing this order."

In 1647 the Town Accounts also show evidence that besides wounds gained through battle, disease was prevalent amongst the soldiers in their tightly packed quarters and often squalid conditions.

"...paid for the buriall of a soldier that died of the smallpox .... 16s. 0d."

8 . CROMWELL'S SPEECH

The Levellers

Public opinion was unfavourable towards an Irish expedition and Parliament faced an army mutiny urged on by the persistent Levellers. The Levellers were extremists whose ideals were reminiscent of some of today's political theories, including the abolition of the monarchy and the House of Lords and that everything was to be owned by the people. In order to gain their ends, they associated themselves in 1647 with the demands of the Army rank and file for arrears of pay and indemnity, and won much influence amongst the agitators.

Speaking at Hyde Park, Cromwell told of proceedings that had been put forward to deal with the soldiers' arrears of pay, which had become a subject of chief concern. The news did not travel fast enough for a mutiny broke out at Banbury, in Colonel Reynolds' regiment, led by a certain William Thompson, a man at one time sentenced to death for disaffection but spared by Fairfax. The mutiny was of short duration for Colonel Reynolds gathered three loyal troops and killed or dispersed the mutineers. Thompson escaped to join another growing mutiny at Salisbury, made up from the regiments of Colonels Ireton and Scrope.

Cromwell now demanded authority from the Council of State to use money originally intended for the Navy to pay off some of the soldiers' arrears. This did not stop the mutinous regiments increasing in number. Armed with information of their whereabouts, Fairfax and Cromwell were sent with two regiments of horse and three of foot, to deal with the threat of a growing rebellion in the south-west.

The first night (11 May 1649) was spent at Alton, where next morning Scrope and some eighty officers joined Cromwell and Fairfax in a council of war, and drew up an appeal to the mutineers to lay down their arms. On May 12 they reached Andover where Cromwell made a fine speech, addressing it to each regiment, appealing to them in the name of unity and discipline and their past service together.

"..That he was resolved to live and die with them, and that he had often engaged with them against the common enemy of this nation,

Oliver Cromwell
engraved by L. Stocks from the portrait by Sir Peter Lely.
(by courtesy of the National Portrait Gallery, London)

so he resolved still to persist therein, against those revolters which are called by the name of Levellers; not doubting but that they would as one man unite, and with unanimous spirits follow him, for the subduing of them, and bringing the Ring-leaders thereof to exemplary punishment."[13]

On Sunday 13 May, Fairfax sent Major White to overtake the mutineers and persuade them to submit. Cromwell sent a message to the mutineers, ahead of White, to tell of mediation and that Cromwell and Fairfax would "not follow with force at their heels." Before White could overtake them, the mutineers had reached Wantage, from where they marched on to Sunningwell between Oxford and Abingdon. There they hoped to meet another regiment but finding only two troops they marched on toward Newbridge. Meanwhile Fairfax and Cromwell hurriedly marched north to Theale near Reading to cut them off in the east. On the 14 May, the mutineers settled for the night at Burford in Oxfordshire.

Cromwell was sent ahead with the cavalry and Fairfax followed. They made the forty-five miles to Burford before midnight and surprised the unsuspecting Levellers, who could offer little more than a scuffle. One man was killed and a large number were taken prisoner, being locked up in Burford Church. Those escaping were left to be arrested by the Justices of the Peace throughout the countryside.

During his short stay in Andover it appears that Sir Thomas Fairfax was made a gift of a sugar loaf as the Town Accounts bear out:-

"payd. Benia. Bradbourne the 12th 1649 for a Sugar loafe given to the Lord General   0.16s.0"

Hospital Built

Better late than never is perhaps the call when we read in the Town Chamberlain's accounts that the town spent £28-15s.-6d for 'building of the Spittle' (or hospital).

Travel on the Lord's Day

During the Civil Wars an Act of Parliament forbad people without legitimate cause from travelling on the Lord's Day. The Constables for the Borough of Andover made a complaint in 1649 that travellers were evading the orders of the recent Act. The County Justices issued an order to the parishes '..to keep true and diligent ward' to see that the Act was obeyed.

Distinguished Visitor

Judge Robert Nicholas was a visitor to the town in 1650 and the Corporation paid for a pottle (flat bottomed bottle) of wine during his stay at the Angel Inn. An important man in the service of Parliament, Robert Nicholas was made a Baron of the Exchequer on Cromwell becoming Lord Protector. He was well loved in the Commons, and as an M.P. spoke out with a 'fiery tongue' especially on the subject of Archbishop Laud. During the 'Penruddock Uprising' he was captured in Salisbury but eventually released, later taking a small part in the trials of the conspirators. At the Restoration, Nicholas was amongst those pardoned under the Act of Indemnity.

"..payd for a pottle of sack at the Angel when Judge Nicholas there .. .. 2s.8d."

Corporation Worries

There are two mentions in the Town Accounts regarding the necessity to repair the Town Hall, which seems to imply that the soldiers were none too careful about their behaviour in the town.

1648 "Payd. for repairing the towne Hall in March 1648 .. .. ii li 19s 2d."
1651 "Payd John Abbott for his worke and for stuffe used in amending the breach made by the soldiers at the town Hall .. .. 0 li 5s 6d."

There are also signs of the financial state of the town. The accounts of 1651 tell of eight loans to the town of £2 each from members of the

56

Corporation: Messrs. Jno. Rutley, Hinxman, Bray, Borde, Elton, Tho. Noyes, Goold and Alex Cooper. In 1656, the Town Chamberlain's accounts mention '...the losse of manie Rentes in the late warres'.

Petty Felonies

The poor of the town lived from day to day, and it was not unknown for a little poaching to be done in order to make ends meet. Unfortunately some were caught and brought before Justices for punishment, one such person being Thomas Buggley:-

"The examination of Thomas Buggley taken before Joseph Hinxman sen. gent and Willm Cooper twoe of the Justices &c., taken 16 die May 1649.

Saith that although 6 poultrie were this morninge about 1 of the Clocke found by the Constables in his howse whereof 2 pickt and thother in their fethers - and all in his howse in bedd, denies that he knewe howe the poultrie came thither and never saw them.

And further that in the morninge about 12 he mett with Mrs. Sewell, Sam and John Sewell, John Tanner and John Pitman att the Angell who all save the women met at Goo. Ellis from whence all went and left him to pay a groate, and he never sawe them or any of them till in the afternoone and then mett with John Tanner and John Pitman cominge to the towne in the marsh about 3 in the afternoone, and soe returned with them, beinge spoken to by them to goe and drincke att Goodales, which he refused and parted with them att St Johns howse, and went home to his owne howse the backe way.

That Tanner came into Buggleyes about 8 att night and all went to bedd about 9.
                                                    signed Thomas Buggley."

Poaching in Finkley Forest

It was not only the poor of the town who resorted to poaching, for we read of several prominent citizens of Andover having a bill of complaint brought against them during 1647.

23 Charles I

"There is a bill of complaint against Andrew Morring of Andover, Yeoman, Thos. Piper of the same, Coller-Maker, Wm. Blake, of Eastenton, Gentm, Jas Hart of thesame, labourer, George Hellyer, Henry Hellyer and Robt Poore of Hurstbourne Tarrant, Gent: Robert Ash, George Merrick, and Jno. Moreing of Andover, Yeomen; and Wm Goldinge of Woodhouse, labourer, being persons of disordered, riotous, and dissolute carriage and behaviour, combining, and confederating themselves together, contrary to the laws, in the Month of June 1644, did associate unto themselves diverse other riotous, disorderly and dissolute persons, to the number of 20 persons or more, being armed and prepared with gunnes, charged with powder and shott, crossebowes, pikes, buckstalls and other unlawful weapons, netts and engines, and also with greyhounds, mastives and fferretts did hunt, chase and kill and destroy or cause to be destroyed two bucks, and did divide the same among themselves and the same persons during the last 7 years had in like manner destroyed 40 bucks, does and fawns, twenty hares, one hundred couple of coneyes, twenty pheasants, ffortie partridges, and other beests and fowles of the forest, chase and warden. And the sd John Moreing usually keeps one or more greyhounds for the purpose of hunting the game, and some of the defendants had destroyed the pound or pinfold of sd forest of Finkeley. They say in answer that they regret His Majesty's Solicitor should have been informed that they are persons of dissolute, riotous and disorderly c a r r i a g e . They deny all the charges but killing 10 or 12 couple of rabbit, which they understood was according to the King's wish, and they are farre better than those whom the defendants conceive to be the Relators."[14]

9. THE COMMONWEALTH

Pledge of Loyalty

During 1650 a bill was passed known as the Act of Engagement. It decreed that all men over 18 were to take an engagement or pledge of loyalty to the Commonwealth '..as established without a king and House of Lords'. The bill was annulled by the Long Parliament in 1660, but an interesting example survives in the Andover Archives:

'Andever in the County of Southn January the 31st 1652
'These are to testifie on the Behalfe of Mr Nicholas Venables of Andever aforesaid in the County aforesaid gent that he did the daye & yeare aforesaid take & subscribe the Engagement that he would be true & faythfull to the ComonWealth of England that the same is nowe established without a kinge or house of Lords before us Phillip Borde gent & Joseph Hinxman gent for as under two of the Justise of the Peace of & in the Burrough or towne of Andever aforesaid Witnes of hande and sealed hereunto on the daye & yeare first above written.
   In the presence of
   Roger Sherfield'.

Prisoners of War

On the 4th April 1653 the Council of State made the order:-
   "One hundred of the Dutch prisoners at Winchester to be sent to Newbury and fifty to Andover: notice to be sent to those that have them in custody and also to the Mayor of Newbury and the Bailiff of Andover to keep them safely till further notice and to draw bills on the Navy Treasurer for their maintenance not exceeding the allowance of 6d. per day."

These prisoners were those taken by Admiral Robert Blake during an encounter with the Dutch navy led by Admiral Van Tromp in February that year, in the battle for sea trade supremacy. They were held in the town prison in Bridge Street, some of the prisoners being sick and wounded.

The bailiffs of Andover duly wrote to the Navy Commissioners for their "disbursements for Dutch Prisoners", but the Commissioners could not find the time to look into the request and passed it on to the Commissioners for Sick and Wounded 'Little Britain'. After passing the application back and forth between government departments eventually the order was made on March 11th 1654:

"To make out a bill for the bailiff of Andover for disbursements for maintaining the Dutch prisoners."

The order was then made on the 15th March to pay over the sum of £50 14s 6d. A short while later Philip Borde, the town Bailiff, made another request to the Navy Commissioners for a further disbursement of £70.

The Andover town gaol was situated at the river bank, near the bridge in Bridge Street (on the site of the former Municipal Buildings). There are many references to it in the town's minutes and accounts books. In 1657, Thomas Russell was appointed jailor '..to save the Town harmless from any loss incurred of a prisoner escaping and to keep the gaol in good repair'.

Appointment of Register

During the Civil War the registration of baptisms and deaths was generally suspended, due primarily to the expulsion of the clergy. Andover was no different to any other town, for there are no records of burials made between November 1648 and October 1653, when a new Register was sworn in. Parliament passed a Registration Act on 24 August 1653 requiring the appointment of an official register in each parish. The Andover register contains such an entry:

"Thomas Marshall of Andover was Chosen per the inhabitants or the maior parte of them According to the Act of Parliament. the twenty-third day of October, 1653, and tooke his oathe to performe the office of Register this tennth of November following,
        Before me
                                        Alexandre Cooper, Bayliffe."

The Act gave the right of registration to local magistrates and banns were frequently published in the market place as the records show:

"John Annats, Thruxton - Elizabeth Collince, Thruxton banns on 3 market days 12th July - 22 Aug 1657 married by John Rutley, Bailiff, 22 Aug. 1657."

Weyhill Fair and the High Steward of Andover

Weyhill Fair, held at Michaelmas (September 25th) was by the mid seventeenth century one of the largest, if not the largest in the south and west of England. It was renowned for the great sales of sheep and cattle held on the downs. There were huge profits to be made from the sales of fodder and stand hirings and the Corporation had made numerous attempts to take control of the fair and its finances. Ownership of the fair was jointly in the hands of The Hospital of Ewelme, near Oxford and Weyhill Church.

The main part of the fair was held on land belonging to Ramridge House of which the Hospital were landlords. The rest of the fair was held on church glebe land, the patrons of which were Queen's College, Oxford. During the period of the Civil War the fortunes of the fair were not great, as was to be expected, but by 1655 the situation was back to normal and a full fair was held. Records of the Court of Pie Powder (or court of dusty feet) exist for the years 1651 and 1655. This court dealt with minor disputes over ownership of articles and short weight etc. and was presided over by the Bailiff of Andover.

In the Council minutes for the year 1654 there is a proposal put to the burgesses for the town that "Lord Richard Cromwell to be high steward of Andover." The proposal was unanimously agreed, and the Protector's son was approached. He consented and was appointed the High Steward of Andover on the 6th July 1654.

The Corporation of Andover attempted to assert its claim to the fair at Weyhill with tenacity and determination. Many agreed that Richard Cromwell's election to the High Stewardship was an obvious ploy to obtain Parliament's sympathy for their cause. A document now in the safe keeping of Queen's College, Oxford adds powder to that argument:

'If the town of Andover insist upon their loyalty & reflections be made on Mr Drake or his predecessors, it may be replyed, that the first time they refused to pay for their standings on Weyhill to the farmer of Ramridge was in the times of the usurpation, or in the years [16]54 and 55; that in those times they put up Oliver's armie in the church & chose Richard Cromwell for their high steward, in expectation (tis said) to get Weyhill fair therby, & they had so great hopes of it then they bought a piece of ground, called the hundred acres, about midway between Andover and Weyhill, to place it on.'[15]

As High Steward, Cromwell was given the right by the town to nominate its burgesses for election to Parliament. It appears he used his right, for soon after he came into office his brother-in-law, John Dunch, was one of the burgesses nominated as M.P for Andover and he was duly elected on the 22nd September 1654. John Dunch did not remain M.P. for Andover very long, and on the 22nd January 1655 decided to sit for Berkshire.

The Commons issued a warrant for the election of another "Burgess for the Town of Andever in the Stead of Mr. Dunk" but no further action appears to have been taken, and the position was not filled until 1659.

State of the Roads

The march of many armies through Andover made their impression on the roads. Several complaints were made to the Corporation and these, together with many others from all over the country, caused central government to take action. An Act was passed in 1654 requiring surveyors to assess the inhabitants of a parish and to hire labour and carts for mending the highways. This act was the first step in the state's recognition of their duty to keep up the roads.

21 April 1642 '..a dangerous way in the high streete between the Angell and the Markett howse and a dangerous way att the lower end of Newstreet, between Paynes howse and Enham Lane.'

3 July 1646. '..the littol bridge in the Marsh going to Shefors being imperfect not sufficient for his Majesties Leag People to pas over.'

Until the 1654 Act, the roads were the responsibility of the Corporation, and it was up to the local Justices of the Peace to ensure that remedial work was done. An entry in the Town Accounts 1638-51 records:

'1650. Payd the mason for amending the 2 Bridgs .. ..
0 li 3s. 0d.'

Watch and Curfew

The Statute of Winchester was issued by Edward I in 1285 and remained in force until 1827. One of its provisions was that the gates of cities, boroughs and towns were to be kept closed from sunset to sunrise, and watch was to be kept there. The law was instituted mainly to prevent vagrants from travelling after curfew and it laid down remedies against the harbouring of felons and concealing of crimes. The Winchester Statute was exercised more and more during the civil war period.

There are several entries made in 'Presentments for Good Behaviour' making reference to the Statute of Winchester. One such entry reads:

'We present Tobias Besar, Beiamin Bunny and Michaell Rutley for neglecting the watch in departing before three o' clock about the Twentieth of August last Contrary to the Statute.'

A curfew was rung in Andover in the seventeenth and eighteenth centuries, and the town accounts contain regular payments to the sexton for ringing the '8 o' clock and 9 o' clock bell'.

Town Plate Hidden

There is a local tale that the Corporation plate and maces were hidden in the river at this period to avoid them being taken by looting soldiers. Attempts to discover their whereabouts have been unsuccessful. The only tenuous evidence to corroborate the story is that the maces used by the last Mayor of Andover date from the Restoration, 1660.

10. RISING IN THE WEST

Rising

Cromwell's Republican army, a source of discontent to most of the nobility and gentry, could only be maintained by a taxation so heavy, it was more than many could endure. Colonel Pride's 'purge' on the M.P.s which lead to the Rump Parliament and the King's execution, outraged the right wing of Parliament, many of whom were Presbyterians. The Levellers had been suppressed but their spirit was not forgotten, and in 1653 Nicholas Armourer, an agent of Charles II, explored the possibility of a rising. By the end of that year a society for organised Royalist resistance was formed, called the Sealed Knot. It was decided that the original members of the 'Knot' had too much at stake to take part in action against the Protectorate, so new members who were radicals seeking a return to Royal rule were brought into it.

Risings were planned, most of which came to nothing, and so a concentrated effort was made. Agents were elected in all areas to enlist support in the provinces. Richard Pyle, a chirurgeon, was the chief Cavalier agent for these parts. There were several meetings of Cavaliers at Salisbury and Compton, in Wiltshire, and at Pyle's house at Wallop. Parliament prohibited horseracing during this period, as it was well known that Cavaliers held 'meets' at them. However, fox hunting afforded a legitimate object for a meeting and hunting is known to have taken place at the end of February 1655, the week before a general rising had been planned.

Charles II had approved the uprising and was ready to sail on the first news of any success. This was not to come for on the night of Thursday, 8th March 1655 - the night planned for the general rising - none of the members of the 'Knot' acted, nor did the Presbyterians, among them Sir William Waller, a former Andover M.P. and Parliamentary general. In the 'Perfect Proceedings', March 15 to 22 1655 it was implied:

> '.. that Lord Fairfax had 8000 and Sir William Waller had 4000 in London ready to join them, and there was to be a rising in every county.'

On the night, people in only half a dozen widely scattered places throughout England and Wales attempted to gather, but not a party of them were in arms by morning. Cromwell had taken prisoner those in Portsmouth and Plymouth before they had a chance to muster. Taunton slept soundly because the leaders of the Somerset Cavaliers, Sir Hugh and Colonel Francis Wyndham had fled. In Hampshire, a group under the leadership of Sir Joseph Wagstaffe had meant to seize the judges assembled at Winchester for the Spring Assizes, but they postponed this attempt for three days, due to the arrival of a troop of horse.

The next time they were not to be deterred, and on Sunday, 11th March 1655 about 100 Cavaliers - some Levellers amongst them - met at Clarendon Park under Sir Joseph Wagstaffe and Colonel John Penruddock. They marched on to Blandford where they enlisted 80 more and then, having waited outside Salisbury for their friends from Andover and other places, entered Salisbury about 200 strong.

Posting a good force on the Market Place, they proceeded to round up all the horse in the city, and at the same time placed a guard on all the hostelries. They apprehended in their beds the Judges of Assize, Lord Justice Rolle and Baron Nicholas, and also the High Sheriff for Wiltshire, Mr John Dove, all of whom were assembled for the Spring Assizes. The jails were opened up to enlist the prisoners, many of whom were debtors. A suggestion was made to hang the judges, but after discussion it was agreed merely to take the sheriff hostage in his night-clothes. Three to four hundred men now rode out of Salisbury towards Blandford, expecting to meet William Seymour, Marquis of Hertford, but he failed to arrive, and neither did the troops of Waller and Fairfax.

Central Government soon dispatched a formidable force after the rebel band led by John Desborough, Cromwell's brother-in-law. A demoralised Penruddock turned towards Cornwall, traditional home of Royalism, after a useless attempt at raising further troops. He was closely followed by Desborough. At South Molton in Devon, a much depleted army rested, and gave the Parliamentary troops a chance to attack. The rebels fought on for three or four hours but were eventually overpowered. Wagstaffe escaped to France, but Penruddock was captured, later to be beheaded at Exeter.

Among those taken were several from the Andover area:
Richard Reeves, of Kimpton, Gent. (mentioned as a Lt. Col.)
Thomas Helliard, of Upton, Gent.

Edward Moreing, of Andover, Weaver
Joseph Moreing, of Andover, Yeoman
Robert Browne, of Andover, Cordwainer
Edward Painter, of Andover, Currier
Richard Miles (or Mills), of Andover, Clothworker
Richard Hyard, of Amport, Gent
Leonard Catkill, of Cholderton, Waggoner
John Williams, of Fyfield, Carter
William Lewington, of Linkenholt, Husbandman

Two of the Andover men, Richard Reeves and Thomas Helliard were hanged at Exeter; the fate of the others seems more obscure, although it was a ruling at the trials that some should be transported to Barbados in the West Indies.

Petition to the Protector

Peter Noyse, a prominent member of the town council and an efficient businessman, was caught out when a certain John Lucas, to whom Blake had allowed goods valued at £75.13s.2d., had been condemned and executed for his part in the Penruddock uprising, without paying his debts. In a petition to the Protector, Peter Blake explains this and asks for satisfaction out of the deceased felon's estate.

> 'I trusted John Lucas late of Hungerford, Berks with goods value 75li 13s 2d but he being in the last insurrection, was condemned at Sarum and executed, so that I must lose the debt without your relief. I beg that those who are to receive the profits of the estate may pay me ....'[16]

Blake's letter was forwarded, together with many other similar requests, to the Treasury Commissioners; after contact with relatives of John Lucas they seized goods, a house and a shop as forfeit on his estate. A further petition was made by Jehosaphat Lucas, appealing against the decision and asking the Commissioners to return the house and shop on payment of the debts.

Loss of Rents

Another indication of the poor state of local finances, besides that of the loans to the Corporation in 1651, is a memorandum in the Town Chamberlains' accounts dated July 4th 1656:

> 'This accompt was read and allowed by those whose names are hereunder subscribed, there remaining nothing due from the within named John Rutley (town treasurer) in regard of the loss of manie rents in the late warrs.'

It appears that many of the Corporation tenants were unable to pay their rents, due probably to a severe depression in trade and that a large number of the men of the town were still in the service of Parliament.

Entry to Tailors' Company

From around 1175, Andover had a Guild of Merchants with a charter granted to them by Henry II. It was run on the 'closed shop' idea, only allowing the merchants who were not members to trade on market days. The Guild became a powerful body, the government of the town, although having no connection with the enforcement of civil and criminal law. In the sixteenth century it became practical to amalgamate the bailiffs and 24 'forwardmen' to form the Andover Corporation.

At the same time the Guild remained in existence and split into separate Companies (or 'misteries'). The fellowships stipulated that all traders who had been living in Andover for one year were 'free' to carry on trade on payment of 6d., and no one else could trade in the town, except at fairs. No one was allowed to open a shop without joining the appropriate company of his trade, and it was to the Tailors Company that a petition of an ex-soldier was referred by the Quarter Sessions Court.

> 'Upon the humble peticon of Thomas Turner of the towne of Andover exhibiteth unto this courte thereby shewing that hee being in the Parliament service and afterwards being constrained to leave the same by reason of sickness made to betake himself to his trade of a taylour which he did use in the towne of Andover by the space

of halfe a yeare untill such time as the Company of taylors there caused him to be suppressed by reason whereof he hath no meanes of subsistens left to maintaine himself and his family. It is therefoe thought fit and ordered that the Bayliffe and Burgesses of the said towne of Andover for the reasons aforesaid do permit and suffer the said Thomas Turner to use his trade of taylor in the said Towne of Andover at the proper costs and charge of the said Baylifs and Burgesses, And alsoe doe give find and allow the said Thomas Turner sufficient and competant maintainance for himselfe and family.

Ordered that Thomas Turner shall use the trade of Taylor in Andover, that the Bayliffes and Burgesses provide for him and his family.'[17]

Quaker Arrested

The Society of Friends, or Quakers as they are usually known, was founded by George Fox around 1648. Their interruption of church services and enthusiasm over personal inspiration soon brought persecution from the Presbyterian Commonwealth. Fox was arrested, and when brought before Cromwell, promised not '..to take up a carnal sword or weapon' against the regime. He was later released and his movement placed under Cromwell's protection. The Quaker movement from there on thrived, although some local magistrates still had recollections of Fifth Monarchists: an extremist group who supported Cromwell until he assumed the title of Protector, when they agitated against him.

On the 9th February 1658, Humphrey Smith was arrested in Andover, where he was the first Quaker to preach. Judge Wyndham committed him to Winchester Gaol, until he would give security for his good behaviour; he remained in prison until after March 1659, whilst there writing several books and compiling pamphlets.

During 1660 Smith was at liberty, and it was in this period that he wrote a book which he called his 'Vision'. It was a remarkable vision of what was to prove the 'Great Fire of London' in 1666, and also of famine and fear, following the appearance of the Dutch fleet.

On the 14th October 1661 at Alton, whilst on his way to visit his son, also named Humphrey, he was once again arrested and committed to Winchester Gaol. There he remained, eventually contracting gaol fever, and died in May 1663.

Members for Andover

For the second Parliament under the Protectorate, Andover did not return a member, although there were two for the short session under Richard Cromwell. On the 4th January 1659, Gabriel Beck of the City of Westminster and Robert Gough of Vernham Dean were returned as M.P.s for Andover.

Gabriel Beck was a solicitor of the Council of State during the Commonwealth, and married Ann the sister of John Dunch, a previous member for Andover (1654/5). The other member, Robert Gough, is thought to have been related to the regicide William Gough, the Major-General in Charge of Hampshire, Sussex and Berkshire, who died in 1679.

11. AROUND AND ABOUT ANDOVER

The Villages

<u>Abbotts Ann</u>

In accordance with the government's Act of Registration (24th August 1653) the parishioners chose their register and record of this exists in the Parish Register:
> 'Robard Gover of abbitsand was nomeneated and apoynted to be Regaistar of the parish and did take his oathe to performe the said office the 24th day of November 1653,
> Witness, Alex. Cooper, Bayliffe of Andever.'

<u>Danebury</u>

There is evidence that during the Civil War period, Danebury was used as a look-out post, for an iron hammer, an anvil and cannon balls have been found on the hill.

<u>Finkley</u>

Richard Cromwell it would appear was working hard at gaining influence around the country and when a survey was made of Finkley Park in 1652 his name crops up again:
> 'We found Richard Cromwell, Esq., Chief Ranger of the Forest of Finkley, who claimeth office as an inheritance, by means of letters patent, but inasmuch as no Patent was shewn to us, we humbly leave the said claim to be made good before the Honble The Trustees and Surveyor General.'[18]

<u>Hurstbourne Tarrant</u>

An interesting event is mentioned in the *State Papers-Domestic* (April 10th 1645). During May 1643 two Parliamentary soldiers, Captain Clark and Major Gunter, intercepted and captured a messenger with a warrant from the King to the Earl of Caernarvon. The warrant contained information as to the whereabouts of some silver plate collected by the King's subjects for the continuance of the war, and for its conveyance to Marlborough.

The Earl of Essex directed Captain Clark to march with 80 horse from Shinwell to Kingsclere, and from there to Chute Forest. About 6 miles out of Andover at Prosperous Farm, the Captain found a parcel of silver plate buried in a barn under a wheat mow, which was valued around £1200. The parcel was taken to Lord Essex at Reading and Captain Clark claimed it as a prize, but the needs of the soldiers obliged Lord Essex to take it. However, the Captain did not go unrewarded, for he was given a rich saddle, again originally bound for the King, and a horse in recompense for his services.

The King later declared that if Captain Clark ever came near him he would 'sit on his skirts' for robbing him of the precious plate.

Kings Somborne

In a letter written at Salisbury on March 28th 1645, complaint was made that 'the Winchester Horse do much mischief not only in Sombourne and Thorngate Hundreds, in Hants, but even as far as Alderbury near Salisbury, carrying off to Winchester divers honest godly men.'

Winchester was Royalist then, a virtual island in a sea of Parliamentary control, and in order to survive it was necessary to make short lightning strikes to gain supplies etc.

Weyhill

A notebook in the possession of Queen's College, Oxford (once the property of the Rector of Weyhill, Dr. Sanderson) records how a servant had hidden his master's money from the marauding soldiers. The event in question refers to the autumn of 1643.

'Henry Tunks told me June 6th 1658 yt in ye troubles when ye soldiers were about, he and Edward Washberd hid in ye Ramridge coppice in a pot Mr.Drake's money viz. 73 or 75li which they had gathered for the sheep coops at ye fair.'[15]

Mr Drake was the tenant of Ramridge House who collected all the fairground rents for sheep coops etc., on behalf of Ewelme Hospice.

Wherwell

In 1645, Lord De La Warr, owner of Wherwell Abbey, petitioned the House of Lords for protection. He complained he had sustained considerable damage by the quartering of both armies upon his tenants and the cutting down of his woods by the soldiers. He had been informed that his house was now to be turned into a garrison contrary to the order for the protection of peers' houses. He then told them that this '.. was likely to spoil the house and be of little advantage to the State by reason of the hills which adjoined it.'

Whitchurch

The Parliamentary army having had the main assault on Taunton aborted, turned and marched for Oxford, on their way quartering for the night at Whitchurch. It was here that a foot soldier was ordered '..to have his tongue bore through with a red hot iron, for notorious swearing and blaspheming, all of which was done for example and terror to others as for justice sake.' The Commander-in-Chief, Sir Thomas Fairfax, often noted for his severity, has also been described as a prudent general.

Local Folk Tales

Such a colourful time in history is bound to bring forth folk tales associated with the period, and although it is realised such tales are merely legends, some may be based on fact. Over the years these stories have been told and re-told and on each occasion some small part of the story has been altered and added to. Facts are gradually swept aside and a different tale is left behind.

The original stories can sometimes be traced through records, but these are few and far between - and so we content ourselves with the idea that there must be some grain of truth for there to be any story at all. These tales of the Andover 'happenings' although seeming far fetched, do give one a feeling of the time, even if a little 'artists licence' has been used.

The Wolversdene Ghost

The daughter of a strict Parliamentarian had fallen in love with a young Royalist soldier quartered in the town. Realising her father would have strong objections, she resorted to seeing her lover after dark, slipping out of the house to meet him. Missing his daughter the father set out one night to find her, and did so, in the arms of her soldier. The father, enraged at the thought of his daughter with one of the enemy, struck at the young Cavalier and killed him. His daughter was sent home to bed, but her grief overcame her and she ran through the house and flung herself out of an upstairs window, screaming as she fell to her death on the flagstones beneath.

The young girl's death was at a large house in the area where The Wolversdene Club now stands. During the Second World War, Wolversdene House was used to house WAAF personnel working up at the airfield. On one occasion two of these women applied for and received a transfer to another base, because they could no longer stay in the house as they had on more than one occasion felt their room go cold, heard footsteps go past them, heard screaming and then a thud.

The Headless Cavalier

Union Street in Andover is believed to be haunted by a headless Cavalier. According to this legend should he point his sword at some unfortunate, it is 'the kiss of death'.

The Ghost of Coombe Manor

A young Cavalier was staying at Coombe Manor, a house having a strong Royalist affinity, when the news was received that the Roundheads were coming for him. Having no time to run, the Cavalier decided to hide up a chimney and clambered up to hang by the fingers just below the top.

The Roundheads searched the house to no avail and turned their attention to the outhouses and stables. One soldier whilst searching on the roof spotted the unfortunate soldier's fingers hanging on to the chimney stack, and he drew his sword and chopped off the fingers of both hands, sending the Cavalier plummeting down. As if that was not enough, the soldiers then finished off the poor man with their swords. The story continues that to this day there is a red blood-like stain in the hearth and a mark on the ceiling of the room below, which despite constant cleaning always re-appears a short time afterwards.

Nether Wallop Legend

There is a local legend in Nether Wallop that during the Civil War the Vicar of St. Andrew's Church hid the church plate in 'Knockwood', the old farmhouse overlooking the marsh, for safe keeping away from marauding Parliamentary troops.

The Penton Mewsey Sanctus Bell

There is a tale at Penton of the sanctus bell which now hangs in the church. It was struck in 1555 to replace a former bell removed during the reign of Edward VI. This bell was also removed when it was heard that Roundheads had started a campaign of destruction in the neighbouring area. It was rediscovered in 1845 by a mason whilst he was repairing the Rectory wall. From then it was kept by the rector, who used it as a handbell in his own house, but it disappeared when he died.

The next rector, Rev. Clutterbuck, an experienced local historian, spent the last few years of his life looking for the bell, but he died in 1896 without finding a trace of it. It was said in the village that some had seen his ghost dressed in a cassock, knocking on the doors of the cottages in his quest, long after his death.

The sanctus bell hangs today in the church, after having been found by the Rector of Penton Mewsey from 1914-1946. He was roused to continue the search after his wife had seen the ghost one night. After considerable research, the bell was traced to the surviving family of a low church rector, who after a protracted correspondence agreed to part with it. From that moment the ghost of the Rev. Clutterbuck is said to have been laid.

Lucky Shot at Wherwell

Dr. M. Gillett in 1917, wrote in a booklet entitled *Folklore, Legends and Superstitious Customs in connection with Andover and Neighbourhood*:

'When Oliver Cromwell was fighting the Stuarts, he fired some cannon balls at Wherwell Priory. Several of the balls, however, fell short of range, and one of them it is said descended the chimney of the White Lion Inn at the foot of the hill, and another at the door. This I think must be partly correct, as under the two inn street lamps are those cannon balls - or are said to be.'

Rivalry Between Villages

Whilst I was researching for this history of the Civil War I have been told many tales which as I have mentioned may have been based on truth. One such is the following.

There has always been a kind of rivalry between the villages of Upper and Lower (or Goodworth) Clatford. It was said that this was due to the fact that during the Civil War, Upper Clatford declared for Parliament, whilst Lower Clatford was for the King. Anyone moving from Goodworth Clatford to Upper Clatford was jeered and called 'Royalist' right up to the early part of this century.

Wayside Hospital

In Vernham Dean there is a house now known as 'Deers Leap' and according to several sources it was used during the Civil War as a Cromwellian wayside hospital. The two storied flint and brick structure is a late 16th century/early 17th century building with unusually large rooms and a high ceiling. On the chimney breast was a plaque (now long since removed) which recorded the fact that it was a wayside hospital during the Civil War.

Among the deeds to the property is a typewritten note stating that it was used as described but giving a little more detail. The house was once known as 'The Homestead'. The real truth may never be known but it may be that wounded were tended there during the local fighting. Strong evidence for similar 'hospitals' exist at Marston Moor and at other battle-sites.

Religious Persecution

Parliament was soon to see that having control of the pulpit was of the greatest social and political importance and after the abolition of the High Commission their aims began to bear fruit. The Church, now firmly under the control of the State, was without any form of church court or link with central government, and in order to fill the vacuum and re-establish some standard of conduct the Major-Generals took charge. Their main interests lay not so much with religion as with security, as can be seen when they prohibited race-meetings where Cavaliers might have met.

In September 1641 the House of Commons voted in a Bill to order the parishioners to set up a lecture, and to 'maintain an orthodox minister at their own charge to preach every Lord's Day where there is no preaching and to preach one day in every week where there is no weekly lecture.' Another bill passed in 1643 ordered ministers to go 'into divers counties ..... to possess the people with the truth and justice of the Parliament's cause in taking up of defensive arms.'

The Commons were very busy ejecting ministers accused of 'scandalous' behaviour and others because of their political attitudes, replacing these with their own specially vetted ministers. In the Andover area alone no less than 32 clergy were ejected, mostly for continuing to use the Book of Common Prayer, which had been abolished in favour of a Presbyterian directory of worship.[19]

A contemporary Royalist newspaper the 'Mercurius Rusticus' often made scathing attacks on the Parliamentarians, particularly on Sir William Waller who had been described as 'that well known plunderer'. It reported:

'About December 1642, the Collonels Waller, Browne, and others, marching from Ailesbury to Windsor, and thens by Newbury to Winchester, their soldiers in the march plundered every minister within six miles of the road without distinction, whether of their own party or of the other, whether they subscribed for Episcopacy, Presbytery, or Independancy, whether they wore a surplass or refused it, only, if they did not they afforded the less booty.'

12 . THE RESTORATION OF THE MONARCHY

The Protector's death in the autumn of 1658 threw the country once again into turmoil. Royalists were crowding into the churches with thanksgiving and all agreed that surely England would summon back its exiled monarch. A coup was planned for 1 August 1659, and Charles went to Calais to be close at hand if it should succeed. But it was not to be. A lack of co-ordination and bad organisation doomed it to failure. The future of the Protectorate seemed secure for the moment, especially when Oliver Cromwell's eldest son Richard was proclaimed the Lord High Protector.

At first Richard was favourably received, but he did not have the confidence or the ability of his father to hold the country together. Unrest in the army grew and tensions rose in Parliament. The Protector even had to be rescued from arrest for non-payment of his debts. He began to lose favour with both Parliament and his people, and with the army's virtual takeover of Parliament, thoughts were turned towards a restored monarchy.

As the year 1660 broke, a strong Royalist feeling was running through the land and it was generally felt the way was now open for consultations with the exiled King. On General Monck's advice, Charles took up residence in Breda and awaited further development. Meanwhile in Scotland, Monck had made his move; he marched south with a strong force, repelling all resistance and presented himself at the capital. His declared intention to call a 'Free Parliament' backed with a 'Declaration from Breda' granting pardon to enemies, promising to uphold the Anglican Church and the payment of arrears to the army, left the Royalists with no doubts as to the outcome. By the spring preparations were in hand for the return of the King to England and a fleet was dispatched to Holland taking with it a chest containing £50,000 as a gift to the King.

On the 25th May 1660, Charles II alighted on British soil amongst a blaze of colour and decorations. Flags flew from every rooftop and the people cheered and celebrated.

Celebrations in Andover

The Town Accounts record a celebration on the 13th May 1660 on the announcement of the famous 'Declaration of Breda', signed on April 14th, and addressed by the King to '...all his loving subjects' and promising a general amnesty.

'Laid out at his Maiestie's proclomation - to the soldiers and other £3..10..0'

Andover celebrated, gifts flowed almost literally, for Mr. Westcombe was paid £7-5-0 for wine and Miss Waller was given two sugar loaves. The bell-ringer was granted 5 yards of a smart grey cloth for a new uniform at a cost of 12s.6d to the town.

One visitor to the town in 1661 was Thomas Clarges, a man who played an important part in the Restoration by carrying Parliament's request for Charles II to return to England. The town laid out a present to him of 30 shillings.

The same year came the Coronation and yet another chance for celebrations. The town this time had its maces remodelled and Mr. Westcombe was paid £7-2-0 for more refreshment. The bailiff was allowed £8-8-0 expenses.

From then on the coronation, like the King's birthday, became a date for rejoicing.

APPENDIX I
CIVIL WAR COMMANDERS MENTIONED IN THE TEXT.

Fighting for the King:

Lord Grandison
Lord Digby
Lord Ogle
Lord Crawford
Lord Hopton
Lord Gerrard
Lord Forth
Lord Percy
Prince Rupert
Prince Maurice
Sir William Ogle
Sir Henry Bard
Sir Edward Stawell
Sir Hugh Wyndham
Col. John Bolle
Col. John Smith
Col. Francis Wyndham
Earl of Sussex (later turned to Parliament)

Fighting for Parliament:

Earl of Essex
Earl of Manchester
Sir William Waller
Sir Thomas Fairfax
Sir William Balfour
Sir Arthur Hazelrig
Gen. Oliver Cromwell
Lt. Gen. Middleton
Col. Richard Norton
Col. William Carr
Col. Henry Ireton
Col. Scrope
Sir Richard Grenville (later turned to the King)

APPENDIX II
REFERENCES

1. Quoted by F. H. Sparrow, The Story of the Rev. Robert Clarke, Vicar of Andover. *Lookback at Andover*, 1990. pp.10-13.

2. Quoted in Melville T. H. Child, *Andover. Money, Men and Manners* (1970). pp. 51-3.

3. References re False Prophet:
    Pseudo Christos, printed by John Maycock. London (1650).
    N. Cohn, *The Pursuit of the Millennium* (1957). pp. 330-3.
    Christopher Hill, *The World Turned Upside Down*. pp. 49-50, 171, 179, 209, 249, 316-7.

4. John Rushworth, *Historical Recollections*. 1659-1701.

5. Both quotations from Rev. G. N. Godwin, *The Civil War in Hampshire*. (1904 edn). p. 44.

6. BL Add. MSS 27,402 f.86.

7. Lord Hopton, *Bellum Civile*; quoted in John Adair, *The Battle of Cheriton*, 1644. (1973). p.33.

8. Edward Walsingham, *Brittanicus Virtutis Imago* (London. June 1644, T.T.E53).

9. Military Papers, 1644; Braborne MSS in Kent R.O., quoted in Adair, *supra*, p.212.

10. Both quotations from Godwin, *supra*, p.271.

11. Quoted in John Adair, *Roundhead General*. (1969). p.168.

12. Sir William Waller, *Recollections* (1788) p.124; quoted in Antonia Fraser, *Cromwell Our Chief of Men* (1973).

13. ed. W. C. Abbott, *The Writings and Speeches of Oliver Cromwell* (1939) Vol. II, p.68.

14. Bill in the Exchequer by the Attorney General, 1647. Quoted by Joseph Stevens, *A History of St. Mary Bourne* (1888) p. 329.

15. Queen's College, Oxford. MS 3V28. Rev. Sanderson's Notebooks.

16. *Cal. State Papers, Domestic.* Vol CL111.1. p.223 (1 Jan. 1656/7).

17. Quoted in Melville T. H. Child, *The Community of Andover before 1825* (1972) pp. 38-9.

18. Quoted in Stevens, *supra*, pp. 330-1. The original Survey is in the H.R.O.

19. Clergy ejected in Hampshire are listed in A. G. Matthews, *Walker Revised. Being a revision of John Walker's Sufferings of the Clergy during the Grand Rebellion 1642-60* (Oxford. Reissued 1988) pp. 179-191.

APPENDIX III
BIBLIOGRAPHY

Published Sources

Abbott, W.C.   - Writings and Speeches of Oliver Cromwell (vol ii), pub. Cambridge, Harvard USA, (1939)

Adair, John   - Roundhead General, pub. Macdonald (1969)

Adair, John   - The Battle of Cheriton 1644, pub. Roundwood Press (1973)

Arnold Jones, R.   - Members of Parliament for Andover 1295-1885, pub. Andover Local Archives Committee (1972)

Ashley, Maurice   - England in the Seventeenth Century, pub. Penguin Books (1973)

Ashley, Maurice   - The English Civil War, pub. Thames & Hudson (1974)

Bedford Miles, Emily - A History of the Village of Hurstbourne Tarrant, pub. Holmes, Andover (1942)

Bennett, A.C.   - The Story of St. Mary's Parish Church, Andover, pub. St Mary's Restoration Committee

Bennett, A.C.   - Things Passed Away, pub. Holmes, Andover, (1918)

Bennett, A.C. & Parsons, Edmund   - A History of the Free School of Andover pub. Parsons, Andover (1920)

Brickell, G.E. & Earney, H.W.   - A Background to the Battle of Andover 1644, pub. Andover Local Archives Committee (1975)

Calendar of State Papers, Domestic Series

Child, M.T.H.   - Andover in Hampshire, pub. Author (1969)

Child, M.T.H.   - Andover, Money, Men and Matters, pub. Author (1970)

Child, M.T.H.   - The Community of Andover Before 1825, pub. Andover Local Archives Committee (1972)

Coleby, A.M.   - Soldiers Run Riot Around Andover:1645-6, Article in Lookback No4, pub Andover Local History Society.

Dictionary of National Biography, pub. Oxford University Press

Earney, H.W.   - Inns of Andover, pub. Amateur Winemaker (1971)

Ellis, Rev. Humphrey - Pseudo Christos, London (1650)

Falkus, Christopher   - Charles II, pub. Cardinal (1975)

Featherstone, Donald - Conflict in Hampshire, pub. Paul Cave (1976)

Fraser, Antonia   - Cromwell, Our Chief of Men, pub. Panther (1973)

Gillett, M.   - Folklore, Legends & Superstitious Customs, pub. Holmes, Andover (1917)

Godwin, G.N.   - The Civil War in Hampshire. (1904)

Hall, Derek &   - Farnham and the Civil War, pub. Farnham Museum
Angela   Society

Hill, Christopher   - The Century of Revolution 1603-1714, pub. Cardinal (1974)

Hill, Christopher   - Reformation to Industrial Revolution, pub. Penguin Books (1969)

Hill, Christopher — The World Turned Upside Down, pub. Pelican Books (1975)

Kirby, T.F. — Annals of Winchester College

The Manuscripts of The House of Lords' Vol XI, 1517-1714, pub. H.M.S.O. (1962)

Ravenhill, W.W. — Records of the Rising in the West, pub. Devizes (1875)

Raper, A.C. — Weyhill Fair, pub. Barracuda Books (1988)

Rogers, Col. H.C.B. — Battles and Generals of the Civil Wars 1642-1651, pub. Seeley Services (1968)

Sparrow, F.H. — The Story of the Rev. Robert Clarke Vicar of Andover - Article in Lookback at Andover, 1990 pp.10-13. pub. Andover Local History Society.

Spaul, J.E.H. — The Bailiwick 1599-1835, pub. Andover Local Archives Committee (1971)

Stevens, Joseph — A Parochial History of St. Mary Bourne, pub. Whiting, London (1888)

Tucker, John & Winstock L.S. — The English Civil War, a military handbook, pub. Arms & Armour (1972)

Walsingham, Edward - Brittaniae Virtutis Imago

Watthews, Elizabeth - History of Andover, pub. Andover Public Library

Wedgwood, C.V. — The King's War, pub Collins (1974)

Wedgwood, C.V. — The King's Peace, pub Collins (1974)

Woolrych, Austin — Battles of the Civil War (1961)

Unpublished Sources

From the Andover Archives (now lodged with the H.R.O.)
Andover 2/QS/2 Presentments by the Jury
       4/MI/1 Minutes of Council Meetings 1642-54
       4/AC/7 Accounts 1638-51
       4/AC/8 Accounts 1656-62
Hampshire Record Office 6/M/67 - Parish Register of Baptisms, Marriages and Burials.

KING ALFRED'S COLLEGE